LEADERSHIP
IN
ACTION

LEADERSHIP IN ACTION

Tough-Minded Strategies
from the Global Giant

HELMUT MAUCHER
CEO, Nestlé S.A.

McGRAW-HILL, INC.
New York   San Francisco   Washington, D.C.   Auckland   Bogotá
Caracas   Lisbon   London   Madrid   Mexico City   Milan
Montreal   New Delhi   San Juan   Singapore
Sydney   Tokyo   Toronto

Library of Congress Cataloging-in-Publication Data

Maucher, Helmut.
    [Marketing ist Chefsache. English]
    Leadership in action : tough-minded strategies from the global
giant / Helmut Maucher.
        p.   cm.
    Includes bibliographical references and index.
    ISBN 0-07-041041-0 (alk. paper)
    1. Nestlé Company—Management.   2. Food industry and trade—
Switzerland—Management—Case studies.   3. Food—Marketing—Case
studies.   4. Strategic planning—Switzerland—Case studies.
    5. International business enterprises—Switzerland—Management—Case
studies.   I. Title.
HD9015.S93N5513   1994
664'.0068'8—dc20   94-11898
                                                                           CIP

First published in the German language under the title *MARKET-
ING IST CHEFSACHE.* Copyright © 1992 by ECON Executive
Verlags GmbH, Düsseldorf, Vienna, New York, and Moscow.

English translation by B. J. Perroud-Benson

1 2 3 4 5 6 7 8 9 0   DOC/DOC   9 0 9 8 7 6 5 4

ISBN 0-07-041041-0

*The sponsoring editor for this book was Philip Ruppel, the editing
supervisor was Alfred Bernardi, and the production supervisor was
Donald Schmidt. It was set in Times Roman by Carol Woolverton
Studio in cooperation with Warren Publishing Services.*

Printed and bound by R. R. Donnelley & Sons Company.

Contents

Preface

This book was written after I had spent almost 30 years working in various management positions, the last eleven as the head of Nestlé S.A. In it, I have compiled the experience and insights from those years, as well as the convictions and principles that have guided me.

You will notice that I have not copied a thing from management textbooks: There is nothing about management theories or the fashions that have so exercised the minds of business leaders—or so plagued us. You will not be able to amuse yourself with new explanations about "cooperative management style" or with new theories on "management by...." Nor will you find here answers to questions about techniques or methods, such as the use of established marginal contributions, how to make better use of computers in management or in work operation; there is no complete list of the elements in Nestlé's marketing mix, nor what a personnel assessment sheet should contain.

This is an extremely personal book from the pen of a practitioner, and you will certainly not agree with all of its contents. I have used "management by objectives," but have never disguised my pleasure in "management by provocation" or "management by interview." Long years of practical experience have led me to the conclusion that, unfortunately, many things essential to ultimate success in management are not to be found in the relevant books, nor are they taught at business schools. In German, *management* is *Fuehrungskunst* ("the art of leadership")—one of the few cases in which the German word is better and more precise than the English one. It is not my intention to question the utility of textbooks, and I will readily admit that I learned a lot from studying business administration and, later, from reading many books on the subject and attending seminars.

I would like this book not merely to stimulate and enrich practicing executives and budding managers, but also to inspire them to achieve personal and entrepreneurial success. In a market economy and in a free society that stresses performance, there is never a reason to stop fighting against resignation or to simply give up. Many years ago I said, "In a market economy . . . the world is divided up anew every day." If, on the following pages, you find hints, pointers, and suggestions for running a market-oriented, responsible business, then this book will have fulfilled its purpose.

HELMUT MAUCHER
Vevey, Switzerland

Foreword

HELMUT MAUCHER: FROM THE ALGAU TO VEVEY

By Hans Ziegler

Former Editor-in-Chief, *Kapital*

Hopefully, the fact that Helmut Maucher later became the head of the world's biggest food company did not disappoint his parents too much. For if Maucher's parents had had their way, he definitely would have taken up a suitable type of local job for a boy from the Algau in those days.

Helmut Maucher was born in Germany in 1927, in the Algau region of southwestern Bavaria, where he also grew up. In his youth he used to dream that he would be a district president (*Landrat*) one day, although all his relatives had been ordinary people, that is, farmers and craftsmen. In the course of time his desire to look elsewhere for professional opportunities increased, since they were not available in his native village. Maucher's parents sustained his hopes and gave him all the encouragement they possibly could to carry out his aims.

At first, however, Maucher stayed in his village, where he attended the public school. He owes a great deal to his primary school teacher, Herr Maichel. Not only did Herr Maichel teach in a lively and interesting manner, but he also readily transmitted his experience of life to his pupils—a great benefit to all of them later. Something far more important to Maucher, because it awakened a lifelong interest, was that Herr Maichel introduced him to music, a totally new aspect of life for him. So, as a boy, Maucher learned to play the violin; later, he played the clarinet in the small village brass band as well. It was also thanks to music (Mozart, Bach, and Vivaldi are his favorites) that Maucher and his wife-to-be met in his native village. The couple has been married for 39 years now; they have three sons.

Although Maucher's relatives came from a simple background, they all did well in school and were very open-minded. Maucher continued this family tradition: After finishing five years of primary school in the German public school system, he was certain he wanted to go on to the real gymnasium, or college preparatory high school. At that time, bright pupils from the country usually were sent to a type of boarding school, Hitler's NPA schools. But Maucher's father objected to those schools and insisted that his son attend the nearest high school in Isny. In spite of the tiring daily trip to school, to this day Maucher is still very grateful to his father for insisting on a nonpolitical school.

After the war ended, Maucher transferred to a different school, the Rupert Ness High School in Wangen. During the postwar period in Germany, life was very simple; and people were quite poor. Despite the difficult circumstances, Maucher does not admit to having been unhappy or even discontented.

It was during this period that he met some impressive individuals who helped to shape his character; for instance, Father Reinhard Kempter, with whom he read and discussed literature that the Nazis had forbidden. Thanks to the influence of this priest, Maucher caught the book virus, and he still reads voraciously.

In 1948 he passed the examinations, which in those days were still held in the rigorous form of the French baccalaureate. After receiving his high school diploma, he was faced with the problem of which career to choose. At the end of 1947, during his final year in high school, a high official in the local government taught a guidance class for the students. After hearing the official conclude that, due to conditions in postwar Germany, there was no future for qualified scientists, Maucher decided to begin a commercial apprenticeship with Nestlé in Eisenharz. At the end of his apprenticeship Maucher was transferred to the head offices of the German Nestlé Company, in Frankfurt. After working there for some time, he also began to study business administration at the Johann Wolfgang Goethe University in the same city, from which he graduated with an MBA in 1958.

I shall only briefly outline the further developments in his professional career. He perfected his gift for management at the International Management Development Institute (IMEDE) in Lausanne, Switzerland. In 1963, Maucher was named head of marketing for the German Nestlé Company, and later head of the new Nestlé subsidiaries, Findus and Jopa. After the latter merged with Unilever, Maucher left Nestlé to become manager of the GEG, the "Wholesale Cooperative of German Consumer Cooperatives" in Hamburg from 1970 to 1972. However, he returned to Nestlé at the company's request to become head of the Allgauer Alpenmilch A.G. in Munich. In 1975, Maucher was named chief executive officer of the entire Nestlé Group in Germany and, in 1980, executive vice president and a member of the executive committee of Nestlé's headquarters in Switzerland. A year later, Helmut Maucher was elected chief executive officer. Since 1990, he has been both CEO and Chairman of the Board of Directors of Nestlé S.A. in Vevey.

"I would like to warn all young people who want to get to the top quickly," Maucher said, "not to concentrate all their professional efforts on promoting their own careers. Time and again, the business world has made it plain that those who do not constantly think about their careers but lose themselves completely in their jobs get ahead much better than those who are too eager to advance their careers."

Another secret of success to be gleaned from Maucher's professional career is that, despite constant daily demands on his time, he never seems to be under pressure, and he manages to remain calm even in the most critical situations. This is the best way to put up with such an exhausting job and to keep working at it for many years. Maucher's family certainly helps him a great deal too, since they give him all the support and understanding he needs for a profession that, of course, demands most of his time.

Maucher devotes his limited free time to his family and to keeping abreast of current affairs; and naturally, he enjoys listening to classical music.

Even though he spends half the year traveling on business, he actually remains a home-loving person, very attached to his native region. The open-mindedness Maucher must bring to his job and his attachment to his native Algau are not incompatible but rather form a harmonious whole.

I have added these personal remarks to Helmut Maucher's book to enable the reader to form at least a rough idea of his personality. Although the American business magazine *Fortune* selected him as one of the best managers in Europe, very little is known about his private life. He never appears in gossip columns and avoids jet set society. Yet, Maucher is sociable and by no means a melancholy person, which makes him sympathetic and credible. No wonder prominent politicians appreciate his advice and seek it out.

Maucher considers life to be a unified whole, a union between professional and family life. He cannot understand people who consider their profession to be a mere means, or tool, to optimize their private lives. In Maucher's opinion, only someone who manages to harmonize both family and professional lives can really be happy. This is the way he has always approached his own professional career.

LEADERSHIP
IN
ACTION

1

Ten Axioms for Business Success

1. *Do the normal, sensible thing first.* Produce marketable products; look after your management, personnel, and customers; check the till. In short, do the obvious: get back to the basics.

2. *Change the criteria for selecting managers.* In addition to professional know-how, managers need creativity and commitment, they need to think more about their responsibilities than about their careers or power games, and they need to be courageous and to have good, steady nerves.

3. *Realize the importance of the lowest levels of management: they represent the company.* For that reason, focus on people and products rather than on systems.

4. *Remember that it's better to take the long view than to seize a short-term advantage.* Proper timing also is important; make rapid, though not always perfect, decisions. Keep three phases in mind:

   □ Recognize what is needed early, *then . . .*
   □ Accelerate the decision-making process, *and finally . . .*
   □ Implement the decisions quickly.

5. *Soberly estimate the possibilities of streamlining and of subsequently implementing the measures.* Adapt corporate structures more rapidly to growth and activity/employment. Do not subsidize nonviable businesses; adapt the work force to new circumstances—both regionally and professionally. Think of a reduction in costs as an opportunity to think about longer-term options and to lay the groundwork for future investments.

6. *Do not overlook renovation in addition to innovation.* Furthermore, innovation should be applied to management, leadership, and organization, as well as to products.

7. *Communication as a means to an end is key.* Of course, actions and facts are more convincing than mere words.

8. *Establish good labor-management relations.* Even though an idyllic peace is unlikely.

9. *Implement a new style of management and new kinds of relations with employees: management commitment and employee involvement.*

And last but certainly not least, the most important single axiom for executives:

10. *Be credible and consistent in word and deed.*

2

Nestlé's Global Strategy

The strategy at Nestlé over the past decade has been governed by a group of basic principles. The conceptual framework has remained in place, even when the specific strategies utilized varied from one period to the next.

These basic principles revolve around three main tenets:

1. Develop and consistently use know-how.
2. Do business while keeping in mind the long term.
3. Consider the human element.

The primary source of a company's internal growth is the creation of new products and the improvement of existing ones. That is why R&D is considered so important at Nestlé. Innovation plays an extremely important role in the Group's growth. For example, in 1938, the discovery of Nescafé opened up a whole new area of opportunity for the firm. Later, considerable technological advances, which substantially improved product quality, were crucial to increasing the popularity and use of Nescafé. In the early 1950s a pure instant coffee, with no carbohydrates added, was developed. This was followed in the early 1960s by a new process for aroma extraction, in the mid-1960s by the discovery of freeze-dried coffee, and finally, at the end of that decade, by the development of the agglomeration process and as a result the production of granulated rather than powdered instant coffee.

Yet innovations also led the firm to question certain fundamental aspects of some of its activities. In the field of dairy products, Nestlé had for a long time specialized in the production of sweetened condensed milk. In the early 1960s it began industrial production of powdered milk, which dissolves easily in hot or cold water and tastes very much like pasteurized milk. Since then, powdered milk has progressively replaced condensed milk. As early as the early 1970s, sales of powdered milk already were greater than sales of sweetened condensed milk. Between 1974 and 1984, sales of powdered milk increased by 50 percent, while sales of sweetened condensed milk dropped by 20 percent.

The other source of internal growth—geographic extension of its activities—is especially important to Nestlé. The limited size of the national Swiss market (with only 6.5 million inhabitants) forced Nestlé to develop its business abroad at a very early stage. By comparison, most big American food companies carry on the main part of their business within their huge home market of 250 million inhabitants.

One of the Group's basic strategies always has been to launch a product successfully in a single market and only then extend its sales (and often its production) into a whole series of other markets. If necessary, the product is adapted to national conditions and tastes.

This growth process is based on the cross-fertilization of markets. For instance, in the beginning, instant coffee was produced only in the firm's factories in Switzerland, France, Great Britain, and the United States. At present, Nescafé is being produced in 30 countries. Although at first Nescafé was aimed mainly at industrialized countries with a coffee-drinking tradition, it gradually became popular in countries with a tea-drinking tradition (e.g., Great Britain and Japan). Consumers discovered coffee-drinking via instant coffee rather than by drinking coffee brewed with roasted coffee beans. Sales of Nescafé also grew rapidly in those countries that produce the raw material: Mexico, Brazil, and the Philippines. Instant coffee has conquered a substantial market share there, alongside roasted coffee beans.

Acquisitions are used to help penetrate new fields or to add to or improve existing market share—but without allowing the firm to become predominant or to oust the competition. Acquisitions also are meant to contribute to the geographic and sectorial balance of the company's activities and to bring in new products and markets, while contributing to the Group's profitability.

However, acquisitions are not considered to be purely financial investments, like the ones conglomerates make. When Nestlé buys a company, it does so because the new activities are of interest to the Group or within a field that does not lie outside its own area of experience. (Nestlé does on occasion enter new areas. That was the case with cosmetics and ophthalmological pharmaceuticals. In such cases the company chooses areas that have certain features in common with its main activities—for instance, marketing and R&D. As a result, Nestlé has intentionally restricted its diversification to a very limited number of fields.)

When the Group extends its food activities, it does so via horizontal rather than vertical integration. For example, Nestlé does not engage in farming or cattle-raising; nor does the Group have any part in food distribution or retailing. Nestlé's entry into the restaurant business in the 1970s was an exception to this rule, but the exceptional situation did not last. The Group later withdrew from this area so as to avoid any possible conflict of interests.

THE ROOTS OF THE STRATEGY

How to truly understand the principles and strategies firmly in place in the Nestlé of the 1990s? Since the company's beginnings in the mid-nineteenth century, new products have been developed, companies have been acquired, and the Group has grown in dramatic increments. Nevertheless, the guiding principles of today's company still can be traced back to Henri Nestlé's small company in Vevey, Switzerland.

Thus, before any management and leadership principles are discussed, let's take a look at the key events that led to the development of the Nestlé Group.

When Heinrich Nestlé, a German pharmacist from Frankfurt, began to distribute his "milk food" in Vevey, Switzerland, in 1866, he could never have known that, 125 years later, his firm would be the largest food company in the world. Today, with its 200,000 employees, 430 factories, and over 50 billion Swiss francs ($35.5 billion) in sales, Nestlé S.A. ranks among the largest companies in the world.

It all began in 1843, when, turning his back on his native city, Heinrich Nestlé (who subsequently changed his first name to Henri), moved to Vevey, Switzerland. He set himself up as a druggist and made his living by selling seeds, mustard, and oil lamps. In 1857 several businessmen from Vevey, including Henri Nestlé, founded a small company to manufacture liquid gas and commercial fertilizer.

Soon afterward, however, Henri was caught up in the Swiss Welfare Movement of the time. The high rate of infant mortality drove him to an ever more intensive and untiring search for a substitute for mother's milk. At last he actually discovered one: so-called "milk food," a type of infant cereal. By means of a special drying process, it was produced out of powdered milk, malted cereal, and sugar. Henri Nestlé's process was novel, in that it preserved most of the nutrients in infant cereal, and it quickly became a success. However, skeptical doctors and merchants blocked production on a larger scale. Since the successful use of infant cereal increased nonetheless and demand inevitably grew, even its harshest critics finally fell silent and production of infant cereal on a large scale was at last able to begin.

In 1874, when 61-year-old Henri—worn out and exhausted—sold his company, it was a flourishing firm and there was a brisk demand for his products. Since he and his wife had no children, he found himself in the position of having to find a worthy successor to carry on his life's work. What he eventually settled on was not a person but Farine Lactée Henri Nestlé, a joint-stock company newly founded to make the acquisition.

The first years after the joint-stock company took over Henri Nestlé's firm were marked by internal reorganization, research to improve product quality, and the development of new groups of products.

The first significant event was the new firm's merger with the Anglo-Swiss Condensed Milk Company, which had been founded in 1866 by two American brothers, Charles and George Page. It had been a fierce rival of Nestlé's for many years. This was followed, in 1929, by the acquisition of three chocolate manufacturers: Peter, Cailler, and Kohler, the company's first step into this sector. Nestlé enlarged its range of products once again with the development of the first usable instant coffee, which came on the market as Nescafé in 1938—a product that would become famous throughout the world.

Current events left their mark on the company, of course. The Great Depression and the two world wars, especially, created immense difficulties for the firm; however, they never managed to throw the Nestlé Company out of gear. While they slowed down the inexorable expansion of the company for a short time, they could not stop it in the long run.

Nestlé's development after the Second World War can be roughly divided into three main phases:

1. *Until the mid-1970s.* Fast internal growth, and a few important acquisitions such as Maggi, Findus, Ursina, and Stouffer
2. *From the second half of the 1970s.* Difficult discussions about fundamental changes in the overall environment, due to the oil crisis and other worldwide economic factors
3. *From 1981.* A new wave of growth; revitalization, rationalization, and strengthened resources, as well as accelerated growth (internal growth combined with an aggressive policy of acquisitions)

Let us first consider Nestlé's position immediately after the war. In 1946, the Nestlé Group already was active internationally: its 107 factories were spread out over all five continents. The firm was doing business in four areas of the food industry, three of which were more or less concerned with milk: milk products in the strict sense of the term (especially sweetened condensed milk), baby food (powdered milk and dietetic products), and chocolate (a sector to which Nestlé originally had been led by milk chocolate). The fourth area, instant beverages, had nothing to do with milk, and Nestlé did not enter that field until after it had invented instant coffee—Nescafé—in 1938.

In 1947, the Group expanded into culinary products, another sector outside milk-based products. Nestlé merged with Alimentana, a Swiss company that produced and sold Maggi-brand soups, bouillon cubes, and spices in many countries. Although this acquisition at first might seem to have been a new one for Nestlé, that was not really the case, for both Maggi and Nestlé products used the same dehydration techniques.

During this decade, although the Group made almost no acquisitions, it grew constantly nonetheless. Sales, converted into Swiss francs, doubled. Expansion on a wide scale took place continuously on every continent; the rate of growth varied, however, depending on the group of products. The Group's two newest categories of products, culinary products and instant beverages, grew the fastest. From 1950 to 1959, sales of instant coffee almost tripled. This purely internal growth led to a substantial shift in emphasis among the various activities of the Group.

During this period, sales in Swiss francs doubled once again. Admittedly, external growth was now making an important contribution to sales. In this period of expansion, the Group concentrated on three things.

First, it wanted to diversify within the food industry. Rather than limiting itself to satisfying merely a few of mankind's nutritional needs, Nestlé wanted to offer a wider range of products.

Second, it seemed proper to expand the number of technological processes it utilized and to offer products prepared using other processes in addition to dehydration.

Third, the Group wanted to become active in those branches of the food industry with the most promising future. As a result, Nestlé made a number of acquisitions and acquired interests in seven product areas. Five of them—frozen products, refrigerated products, natural mineral waters, California wines, and restaurants—were popular at the time and seemed to promise exceptionally high potential for growth.

The seven product areas were the following:

1. *Canned goods.* The British firm of Crosse & Blackwell (canned soups and baked beans) was acquired in 1960; in 1963, an interest in Libby, McNeil & Libby (canned fruit, vegetables, and meat) in the United States; due to circumstances rather than any specific intent, that interest was constantly increased and reached 100 percent in 1976.

2. *Ice cream.* Nestlé, together with French partners, founded France-Glaces in 1960; in the same year acquired an interest in Jopa in Germany and, in 1963, in Delasa in Spain. Later, Nestlé took over both companies.

3. *Frozen foods.* An 80 percent interest in Findus International, a Swedish firm, was acquired in 1962 (100 percent in 1969); at the time, Findus was active principally in Scandinavia and in England. The Stouffer Corporation, an American firm, was acquired in 1973.

4. *Refrigerated products.* A minority interest in the French firm Chambourcy (yogurts and desserts) was acquired in 1968, with the intention of expanding its activities abroad later.

5. *Mineral water.* A minority interest was acquired in Vittel in France in 1968. Deer Park in the United States was acquired in 1969, Allan Beverages in Canada in 1970, and Blaue Quelle in Germany in 1974. The well-known brand Perrier was acquired in 1992.

6. *Restaurants.* Eurest, the European Restaurant Company, was set up as a cooperative company together with Compagnie Internationale des Wagons Lits et du Tourisme in 1970; a majority interest in the Cahills chain of restaurants in Australia was acquired in 1971. The two reasons Nestlé entered the restaurant business were (1) the gradual change in eating habits—more and more meals are being eaten outside the home—and (2) a desire to gain direct experience producing for the mass market.

7. *California wines.* Vineyards and the Beringer-brand wines in the United States were purchased in 1971.

THE FORCE OF GROWTH

The expansion of the Group's activities continued in 1971, when it merged with Ursina-Franck, a Swiss company active in many countries and in three chief areas: milk products, baby food, and culinary products. Nestlé felt that merging the two groups would give rise to substantial synergies, mainly in production, distribution, and sales (especially exports, in view of the stiff competition). We later saw that this was true.

And finally, the third means of external growth on which the firm decided to concentrate was diversification outside the food industry. This refers to the French L'Oréal Group, one of the world's biggest manufacturers of cosmetics and hair-care products. The majority of L'Oréal's capital is in the hands of a French holding company, Gesparal Holding, in which Nestlé has had a 49 percent interest since 1974. Mrs. Liliane Schueller Bettencourt, the daughter of L'Oréal's founder, owns the remaining 51 percent.

Nestlé's interest in L'Oréal was a means of preparing the company for long-term growth. Of course, the cosmetics and hair-care industry differs from the food industry; however, since both industries produce products for the human body, the starting point was similar from a marketing point of view. The prospects for growth were very favorable. In short, L'Oréal was an exceptionally welcome partner for Nestlé.

Although, from 1960 to 1974, the Nestlé Group expanded greatly through external growth, it should not be forgotten that internal growth continued as well. Sales of instant coffee, in particular, developed quickly. From 1960 to 1974 the volume of sales of Nescafé quadrupled. Afterward, growth slowed. The actual increase in Group sales from 1975 to 1980 amounted to 20 percent.

In the course of the 1970s, the world's economic condition deteriorated drastically, with far-reaching results. The first oil crisis marked the end of a long period of rapid, regular economic growth; it was followed by years of recession. The number of those unemployed in countries belonging to the OECD rose from 3.5 percent of the working population in 1974 to 5.1 percent in 1975. The unemployment rate reached 5.7 percent in 1980. The industrialized countries were confronted with double-digit inflation. Some developing countries found themselves plagued with galloping inflation; for example, in Brazil the annual inflation rate rose from 15 percent in 1972-73 to 80 percent in 1980.

After the U.S. dollar stopped being convertible into gold, world exchange rates became destabilized and all foreign currencies were devalued compared to the Swiss franc. From the end of 1974 to the end of 1980, the pound sterling, the French franc, and the U.S. dollar depreciated 32 percent with respect to the Swiss franc, while the German mark lost 15 percent of its value.

Finally, the prices of two of Nestlé's most important raw materials soared. From 1975 to 1977 the price of coffee beans quadrupled, owing to the frosts that had blighted Brazilian coffee plantations in July 1975. As a result of additional imbalances between supply and demand, which had begun a few years earlier, the price of cocoa tripled over the same period.

In the second half of the 1970s the internal growth of the Nestlé Group continued; this was especially apparent in the developing countries. Demand for Nestlé products was stimulated by a basic improvement in the purchasing power of some third world countries— among which were both oil-exporting countries and countries enjoying rapid development, thanks to foreign loans. The Group made special efforts to develop its activities in those countries.

During this period, external growth played a secondary role at Nestlé. The overall economic situation did not lend itself to acquisitions. Above all, however, the considerable increase in the price of raw materials tied up a great part of the Group's funds as "working capital." Therefore, Nestlé's freedom of action was seriously limited.

In keeping with its policy of making acquisitions, in 1977, Nestlé purchased Alcon Laboratories, Inc., a firm specializing in ophthalmic pharmaceuticals and instruments for eye surgeons. This acquisition was the result of Nestlé's strategy of geographic diversification. Nestlé's operations in the developing countries were growing faster than in the industrialized world. To prevent these differing rates of growth from gradually leading to a disproportion in favor of third world countries in the Group's total sales, counterweights had to be provided. So Nestlé decided to acquire some rapidly growing companies in the industrialized world. Acquiring Stouffer's frozen foods in 1973 and an interest in L'Oréal in 1974 were previous steps in this direction, so the acquisition of Alcon was yet another step along the same path.

The fact that L'Oréal had begun to take an interest in pharmaceuticals (Synthelabo) contributed indirectly to acquainting Nestlé with this field. Nestlé chose Alcon, the market leader in its specialized area; it had an excellent profit ratio and was growing very fast. Later, Nestlé was able to help Alcon by financing other acquisitions in the same field. These successive acquisitions enabled Alcon to round out its activities and to continue to expand outside of the United States, primarily in Europe.

The Nestlé Group actually acquired several firms that produced ophthalmic medicine, starting with an American company, Burton & Parsons (contact-lens solutions) in 1979.

During the second half of the 1970s, Nestlé was confronted with serious problems that had to be overcome. In industrialized countries, Nestlé was faced not only with a probable long-term reduction in the expansion of demand (a population growing more slowly, a shrinking part of private income being devoted to food) but also with a deterioration in the economic situation and tougher competition in every market.

In many countries, Nestlé's profits were adversely affected by these facts. Rapid growth in the developing countries, amid unsettled and unstable economic conditions, was risky. For instance, in 1980, sudden losses in Nestlé's subsidiary in Argentina led to a sharp drop in consolidated net profits, which fell from an average of 3.7 percent of sales in the two preceding years to 2.8 percent. From 1981, Nestlé implemented a two-step strategy to strengthen the Group's reserves: first internally, by improving its profits and financial situation, and second externally, by making important acquisitions.

Healthier profits were achieved mainly by divesting itself of a series of firms. The Group wanted to remove from its range of products those to which the manufacturer added only a small value and which were thus too interchangeable. This was why, in 1982, Nestlé sold Libby's, a firm producing canned fruit and vegetables. The Group also divested itself of companies that were making continual losses and seemed unlikely to improve. For example, in 1982, a company Nestlé owned jointly with Besnier first bought the French cheese manufacturer Claudel-Roustang; Nestlé then sold it outright to Besnier in 1985.

Businesses that hindered rather than encouraged the Group's growth were sold off. Since 1981, Nestlé has gradually been selling its various interests in the restaurant business, for the Group is now trying very hard to expand sales of its special products for food service, mainly to restaurants. It would have been illogical to continue running the risk of a conflict of interests, that is, of competing with the very restaurants it wanted to gain as customers for its products for food service. Furthermore, the Group examined its range of products in several countries, with a view to concentrating more on those for which demand was strong while dropping borderline products and those for which demand was weak.

Profits were improved by streamlining the organizational framework and methods. The Group's productivity really needed to be improved. Having high-quality products to sell is not sufficient for success in markets where competition is stiff; the products also have to be properly priced. In order to do this, costs have to be carefully controlled and kept as low as possible.

Between 1980 and 1984, as sales increased, Nestlé reduced the total number of its employees by 10 percent. This enabled the company to reduce its production costs and overheads in relation to sales. At the same time, at the top, Nestlé's management style became more flexible and less dogmatic. Processes were revised and simplified, so that executives could concentrate on essential aspects when making decisions and overseeing results.

In order for the Nestlé Group to regain its freedom of action, it was vital that its financial situation become healthier. The company concentrated, above all, on its working capital, which had been increasing constantly, and which tied up an inordinately large amount of capital. Drastic measures were taken that made it possible to reduce stocks and outstanding debts. By 1983 both of these items had fallen off substantially, not only in percentages of turnover in comparison with 1980 but also in absolute figures—and this despite increased sales. Investments remained modest between 1981 and 1983, and the Group spent only small amounts on acquisitions. A marked growth in cashflow and, at long last, more flexible and thus more efficient financial management contributed greatly to improving the firm's cash situation.

The success of these efforts soon became apparent. Net profits rose from SFr. 683 million ($484 million) (2.8 percent of sales) in 1980 to SFr. 1487 million ($1054 million) (4.8 percent of sales) in 1984. The Group's liquid assets doubled, amounting to SFr. 6 billion ($4.2 billion) at the end of 1984, in comparison to SFr. 3 billion ($2.1 billion) at the end of 1980. Simultaneously, the firm's bank loans were reduced to SFr. 3 billion by the end of 1984, whereas they had amounted to SFr. 4 billion ($2.8 billion) at the end of 1980. Thus, at the end of 1984, the Nestlé Group showed a positive balance of interest of SFr. 3 billion ($2.1 billion), compared to a negative one of SFr. 1 billion ($71 million) at the end of 1980.

IMPROVING COMPETITIVE POSITION

These results were obtained without at all endangering the Group's potential for expansion in the middle or long term. On the contrary, while these measures were being implemented, Nestlé also redoubled its efforts to improve its competitive position. These efforts mainly focused on marketing and R&D, the development of specific products, and, finally, on some aspects of the Group's internal organization.

From 1982, marketing budgets were substantially increased. This was done not so much to promote increased sales, which often are only temporary, but rather to promote classical advertising, which builds up an image of product quality, thus safeguarding a lasting consumer preference for our products. At the same time, from 1982, increased sums were devoted to R&D in order to improve Nestlé's existing range of products and to develop new products for the future. In 1982, Nestlé laid the cornerstone for its research center in Vers-chez-les-Blanc, near Lausanne.

During this period, the Group began to implement new product policies aimed at the future. Three of them are worth mentioning here. In the past, Nestlé had limited its interest in the coffee sector to instant coffee, because instant coffee sold well and made high profits. It hardly seemed lucrative to move into the sector of roasted coffee beans, since profits generally were lower there. New trends became apparent in several countries, however. Because electric coffee machines had become widely available, many consumers were turning back from instant coffee to brewed coffee. Therefore, Nestlé decided to begin selling roasted coffee beans, but to limit itself to special types of beans only. Here Nestlé's experience in purchasing (choice of qualities), in roasting processes, and in marketing all proved to be extremely valuable. Moreover, this increased the company's ability to compete with its main rivals, which were already selling a whole assortment of coffee products, from instant coffee to roasted coffee beans.

In some countries (Great Britain, Japan), Nestlé already had been selling roasted coffee beans under its own brand name; in others, the Nestlé Group preferred to acquire firms that already sold roasted coffee beans. In past years, promoting chocolate sales had not been among Nestlé's strategic priorities, and the Group had barely begun to exhaust the potential of this product. Then, Nestlé decided to become more active in this area: in R&D, marketing, and the creation of new products. The company also decided to strengthen Nestlé's presence in the United States. By 1984 all of these goals had been reached, thanks to internal development and acquisitions.

Nestlé had had an interest in food service for a long time; however, here too it had not taken advantage of the sector's full potential. So steps were taken to develop this business further in the future, especially by producing special products for bulk consumers and institutional customers.

In addition to reinforcing marketing, R&D, and product development, Nestlé also adapted its internal organization and methods in order to help introduce and implement its strategies for expansion.

At Group headquarters, some departments (for example, the one studying possible acquisitions) were dropped, while in other departments (that is, those responsible for groups of products) new aspects of jobs were emphasized. There was a need to concentrate more on projects for the future than on running current business—really a job for operating companies in the markets. Nestlé's long-term planning process also was considerably modified, formal requirements especially (less detailed financial forecasts), so as to encourage a climate of innovation among those responsible for specific markets, to stimulate discussions, and to examine possible alternatives in more detail.

After having improved its profits and financial situation between 1980 and 1983, Nestlé once again was able to consider making acquisitions so as to fulfill many of its objectives. First, selected takeovers would enable the Group to strengthen its position in a specific country or range of products, which would in turn increase its ability to compete. Moreover, Nestlé wanted to increase its presence in the United States (the free world's biggest market, as well as one with an enormous potential for expansion) through acquisitions. In 1983, Nestlé's sales in the United States amounted to a mere 19 percent of its global turnover; furthermore, Nestlé's business in the United States (where sales amounted to a mere $2.5 billion) was too small to compete successfully against its much bigger rivals.

Small and medium-sized firms with a confirmed ability to innovate and specific know-how that Nestlé still lacked were targeted for these acquisitions. With Nestlé's financial support and worldwide sales organization, the Group would be able to contribute to developing those firms' business abroad. Nestlé also would consider acquiring food companies with very good brands that could be introduced into other countries. A further objective was to strengthen the Group's non-food divisions (ophthalmological pharmaceuticals and cosmetics) through acquisitions.

Nestlé wanted to become more active in the area of chocolate and roasted coffee beans. External developments complemented the Group's internal efforts. For example, the Group took over the American chocolate manufacturer Ward Johnston in 1984. In the same year it also acquired two companies that specialize in catering to institutional customers: Paul F. Beich (in the United States) and Goodhost Foods (in Canada). The former sold chocolate, and the latter chiefly roasted coffee beans. In 1985, Nestlé took over two producers of roasted coffee beans in the United States: Hills Brothers and M.J.B.; it also acquired an interest in a German manufacturer of roasted coffee beans (Dallmayr) as well as one in Spain.

EXPANSION IN THE UNITED STATES

The Nestlé Group utilized a favorable opportunity to expand its interests in the field of cosmetics. In 1984, Nestlé acquired Warner Cosmetics in the United States and merged it with Cosmair, Inc. (L'Oréal's subsidiary in the U.S.). Thus, Nestlé acquired a majority interest in Cosmair. Today, Cosmair is one of America's leading cosmetic, skin-care, and perfume companies. To ensure maximum efficiency in this very specific area of business, Nestlé signed a contract entrusting L'Oréal with managing Cosmair. In 1994, the Cosmair shares were transferred to L'Oréal and the Cosmair operations became fully consolidated affiliates of the L'Oréal group.

In the field of ophthalmological pharmaceuticals and optical instruments, Nestlé made a takeover bid for Coopervision in the United States, in order to expand Alcon's business considerably. Unfortunately, the conditions the Federal Trade Commission imposed before giving its authorization would have virtually negated all of the acquisition's advantages; so Nestlé decided to abandon it.

The biggest company Nestlé acquired in America was Carnation. Carnation had sales of approximately $3.5 billion (three-fourths of those sales made in the U.S.). It principally sells milk products and instant beverages, culinary products, and pet food. In September 1984, Nestlé made a public offer of $3 billion for Carnation; the takeover was formally completed in January 1985. Nestlé's main reason for acquiring Carnation was to strengthen its presence in the United States.

LONG-TERM PROSPECTS

It is essential that the Nestlé Group maintain its ability to sell its products successfully and to earn a satisfactory profit from them over the medium and long term. There can be no question of maximizing short-term performance at the expense of long-term potential. This is a fundamental Nestlé principle. Admittedly, being a Swiss company has its advantages in this regard. American companies, by contrast, are forced to publish quarterly results. Any variation of only a few cents in profit per share over one three-month period is considered very important by financial analysts and investors on Wall Street. Therefore, many companies are tempted to resort to expedients that will enable them to publish favorable quarterly results—whatever the company's situation may be. They may, for example, suddenly cut down drastically on advertising. There have even been occasions when a company has sold some of its most profitable businesses so as to produce a book profit on the sale. Such expedients often adversely affect a company's long-term potential.

Nestlé considers it very important to keep its activities and, even more, its risks evenly distributed. It might be tempting, in the short term, to allow imbalances to arise, or even to promote them. It would be conceivable to concentrate a big proportion of the Group's resources on a product (or a country) that was doing very well at a specific moment. In the long run, however, that would mean exposing the entire Group to a single specific risk.

The most important thing for Nestlé is to try to maintain some sort of balance between its products. Nestlé has made sure that it is not excessively dependent on instant coffee; thus, coffee has tended to form an increasingly lower percentage of the Group's total profits. This was not the result of a drop in the absolute value of coffee's contribution to Nestlé's profits but rather the result of higher profits achieved by other categories of products. The latter grew very quickly, improved their profitability thanks to rationalization, or were expanded with the help of acquisitions.

One of the firm's long-term goals is to establish a geographic balance, not so much in terms of individual countries as in terms of large areas of the world such as Europe, North America, and Africa/Asia/Oceania/Latin America, or between industrialized and developing countries. The Nestlé Group first began expanding in Europe more than a century ago, and it is now firmly established there. Yet in some European countries the rate of growth has slowed, and competition often is very fierce. The United States forms a vast unified market, as opposed to a fragmented one like Europe's; and some niches in the American market still have great potential for growth. However, the U.S. market also is a difficult one, and successes and failures tend to match it in size.

Lastly, the other continents contain only a few developed countries: initially, the third world countries had fast-growing markets; today, because of their foreign debts, some of them have been forced to implement harsh measures of austerity. In addition to the structural risks (for example, of full or partial nationalization) in these countries, a new series of new risks—or, where they already existed, worse ones—and uncertainties has been added, due to economic difficulties: restrictions on imports and monetary transfers, huge devaluations, blocked or strictly controlled prices, along with the continuing inflation of costs. Luckily, in the past few years, free-market forces gradually have made themselves felt more and more.

In view of Nestlé's goal of maintaining and strengthening its long-term potential, the company's financial situation is of fundamental importance, for the Nestlé Group's capacity for action depends largely on its finances. Cash must be readily available when action is called for; capital must not be tied up where it is not essential. This means strictly controlling stock and debtors, and centralizing cash as much as possible so that it really is available rather than scattered throughout the Group.

Having a sound financial situation provides a company with an adequate margin for maneuvering. This in turn makes it possible to finance acquisitions on a sound basis and, once they have been completed, to concentrate on integrating the companies taken over and on developing them for the future. By contrast, in the late 1980s some American firms without sufficient resources took over very large companies. This forced them to hurriedly sell off a major part of the activities of the companies they had taken over, in order to try to reduce debts, which had become excessive. In such cases, management has to concentrate all its efforts on these resale operations, which leaves insufficient time and energy to successfully integrate and manage the firm taken over.

However, it would be wrong to confuse concern about a sound financial situation with ultraconservatism: a sound financial situation is a means of action, not an end in itself. Thus, Nestlé's large liquidity enabled it to contemplate taking over a firm the size of Carnation, although that acquisition meant accepting a temporary increase in debt to cover part of the acquisition's cost.

In a firm like Nestlé, the human factor plays a prominent basic part in company strategy. It is essential (in order to achieve customer satisfaction) to give priority to people and products rather than to systems. This includes preparing selected executives to replace holders of key positions within the Group later on. It means making the necessary decisions, well in advance, regarding the selection and training of future executives. Moreover, Nestlé tries to fill its leading posts by internal promotion as much as possible, rather than by recruiting from outside the firm. This helps to ensure a degree of unity, and allows options to be ventilated at an earlier stage.

The human aspect also plays a much bigger role than commonly believed when companies are being acquired. Integration has a better chance of being successful if the two firms' ways of thinking and acting—their "corporate cultures"—are similar. Success also depends on how well the acquisition is accepted by the top people in the company being taken over. This is why it is exceptional for Nestlé to make a hostile takeover bid. Both Rowntree and Perrier were up for sale; the question was not whether there would be a takeover, but merely who would take the companies over. Once an acquisition has been completed (for instance, at Perrier in 1992), Nestlé applies the following philosophy:

1. Work together with the management of the other companies.
2. Give all employees the same chances.
3. Refrain from enforcing Nestlé methods brutally.
4. Have staff departments act with restraint.

Lastly, it is important for a multinational company to adapt to local conditions, as well as to the traditions and mentalities in each country, while safeguarding the Group's basic principles and interests. Nestlé's guiding principle is always the same: Only the best is good enough.

CONTINUITY AND FLEXIBILITY

I have explained the basic principles underlying Nestlé's strategy for growth, but it seems useful to define the concept of a business strategy itself. To function efficiently, a company must be flexible. A genuine strategy can never be a straitjacket, a dogmatic program that invariably forces the firm to make decisions according to a pre-established code. Nor can it be a simple catalog of high-sounding precepts, whose only conceivable use would be as slogans designed to delude public opinion.

Business strategies and their implementation often depend on what might be termed "the burden of history": a big company over a hundred years old cannot disregard the past and act as if everything were starting anew; its roots run deep. Therefore, having a business strategy does not consist in defining what should be done in an ideal situation; it leaves enough scope for flexibility: changing what is wrong in the present situation, entering new fields, disposing of existing businesses. When necessary, Nestlé can even "change its spots."

For instance, in the course of the past few years the company has agreed to several joint ventures, even though Nestlé usually prefers to develop alone and at its own risk. When a joint venture provides a better—or the only—solution, however, Nestlé is open to it. In the companies jointly owned by Nestlé and Coca-Cola (instant beverages based on coffee and tea), Nestlé and Baxter Healthcare (clinical nutrition), and Nestlé and General Mills (breakfast cereals), the advantages of partnership so clearly outweighed those of going it alone that they overcame any misgivings.

Periodically, business strategies must choose among different branches along the roads to various goals; therefore, it is illusory to think that plans can be applied blindly or mechanically, without taking unexpected developments into account. When an opportunity arises—sometimes quite by chance—strategic principles can help management to decide whether or not it is right to seize that opportunity. This was the case in Nestlé's acquisition of Buitoni, the world-famous Italian manufacturer of pasta. When the opportunity to acquire Buitoni presented itself, the fact that Italian cooking corresponds nicely with the long-term trend in eating habits—the replacing of animal protein with vegetable protein—was taken into consideration.

Strategies imply flexibility, and Nestlé's decentralized organization gives its operations that needed flexibility. Where important decisions are concerned, it is important to draw the proper conclusions from mistakes that may have been made in the past, and to correct what can be corrected as soon as possible.

Isn't strategy ultimately the art of controlling change rather than being controlled by it? Nestlé intends to continue in its internal growth. This will mean closely watching the evolution of consumer requirements, and developing new technologies to better satisfy those requirements. The crucial criteria for food products are nutrition, quality, convenience, and freshness, as well as the relationship between quality and price.

Finally, Nestlé's wave of growth in the industrialized countries, not least owing to its large acquisitions, in no way means that the company now accords only secondary importance to third world countries. On the contrary, Nestlé is trying to extend the production and sale of food products—once the prerogative of the industrialized countries—step by step, to a great many of the developing countries. Increasingly, the Nestlé Group is developing products in keeping with local tastes, producing them with raw materials available on the spot, and selling them cheaply enough so that most people in the third world can afford them. Nestlé's research centers, one in Latin America (Ecuador) and the other in Asia (Singapore), are actively engaged in this task.

Having increased its sales over the last 40 years by a factor of 16 (in constant Swiss francs), Nestlé's sales now exceed SFr. 50 billion ($35.5 billion). One might well wonder whether Nestlé's size is still reasonable; whether there is a real danger of "gigantism." Nestlé's size would indeed constitute a problem under three circumstances:

1. *If the Group had become unmanageable.* This is far from true of Nestlé, since it has a quite widely decentralized organization.

2. *If the Group's presence were out of proportion to its environment and too cumbersome for it.* In fact, Nestlé's sales, activities, and factories are scattered throughout the world, and the average Nestlé factory has 250 employees (although the biggest one does employ 4000).

3. *If Nestlé's size had led to a monopoly situation.* This too is far from the case. The Nestlé Group faces stiff—sometimes even fierce—competition in its markets; from our perspective, this has a beneficial effect, for competition brings consumer and company interests into line with one another and thus is a source of progress.

3

Marketing
Is a Job
for the Boss

Practicing the art for the art's sake is not what is needed in marketing; rather, companies need to rethink what marketing should really achieve. Companies need to develop interesting, attractive products that consumers will like and that provide a service. Then they need to create good advertising for those products and to sell them to consumers at competitive prices, which will enable their businesses to make a profit.

One's attitude toward marketing—more precisely, having a marketing sense that constantly reminds one of the commercial purpose of marketing—must therefore take priority over any and every marketing technique. Too often marketing is confused with marketing techniques, which are nothing more than useful aids. For this reason, market research, analyses, calculations, checklists, and sales techniques must be kept in their proper, useful place and should never be confused with the actual development, production, and sale of goods and services—which are, after all, the essential aspects of true marketing.

Marketing is a job for the boss. This important fact is not always understood by employees and marketing experts—at Nestlé or at other companies for that matter. Young marketers want to be the ones who make the decisions on marketing, strategies, products, advertising, and capital investments. Sometimes it is necessary, even if painful as well, to tell junior executives that certain aspects of marketing really are a "job for the boss," and for the following reasons.

□ *Marketing must be a part of general corporate strategy; there is no such thing as isolated marketing.* At Nestlé, for example, long-term investments are made in the market, in products, in personnel, and in factories. We build and expand capacity based on marketing goals, incurring risks that must be looked at in the light of long-term profitability.

29

☐ *Marketing is sometimes linked to acquisition policy.* In recent years, Nestlé has made a number of acquisitions for strategic marketing purposes. We did not make these acquisitions like portfolio managers, who want to invest money. Rather, we weighed the marketing factors with great precision. We looked for market share with a potential for growth that could be promoted better through acquisitions than through internal marketing programs. Growth programs and geographic expansion also are clearly a job for the boss.

☐ *Some risks a company incurs and investments it makes can have far-reaching consequences.* No responsible CEO should let these crucial corporate affairs out of his or her hands. Delegation is possible to a certain extent, but product design and quality as well as communication, advertising, and contacts with major customers—all of them aspects that represent the company in the market—are as a rule difficult to delegate.

☐ *Delegation is preferable when it is possible.* It's favored at Nestlé, because we want to remain flexible and decentralized, but there are areas that must be supervised by the boss and the boss only. During my many visits to our markets around the world, I look not only at our employees but also at our products. I taste them; I examine our packaging, our communications, our advertising for the products; and if at all possible I always try to visit stores and to keep in touch with our major customers. Reports and figures can be read at home; I don't need to fly to Brazil for that.

☐ *Marketing is a job for the boss and top management, because continuity is important.* For instance, changes take place in companies through job rotation. The people who run the company, the top managers, are the ones who embody continuity. They have more experience, and therefore a better understanding of the crucial importance to customers of that continuity and confidence that is built up only over the long term.

Executives should devote most of their time to these "boss's jobs." When priorities have been properly identified, they must be ready to personally put in the necessary time dealing with these crucial aspects of marketing. That is the only way that marketing can contribute to corporate success in the long run.

MARKETING IS MORE THAN TECHNIQUE

In an increasingly competitive economy, everything becomes harder. The fight for survival intensifies, and that inevitably encourages short-term thinking and actions. In addition, many ambitious employees hope to make their mark quickly and thus are inclined to think and act with a view to the short term alone. Or they let themselves be guided by what is fashionable, or chic, in marketing, confusing short-term trends with real, long-term successes.

Obviously, this kind of short-term thinking is wrong. If, for example, Nestlé wants to be successful in the long run, it must force itself, again and again, to concentrate on long-term prospects. When Nestlé does something today, it must take into account what the implications will be for the company in 5 or 10 years' time. One example is the old question of "push" and "pull." Our salespeople and promotion experts keep urging us to spend more money over the short term to push goods into the stores. They are less concerned about seeing to it that consumers take those goods out of the store over the long term.

Increasingly, managers also are inclined to compare quality and costs, and to concentrate on costs alone. They agree to compromise on quality and to carry out value analyses, which always slice away at quality in hopes of improving the cost picture. The long-term results of such "salami" tactics are poorer-quality products and a dwindling market share.

Another trend with transitory effects is discounting, and similar compromises to increase sales in the short term. All marketers occasionally make temporary concessions so as to salvage monthly sales figures. This is a mistake from a long-term point of view: the seller must demand the proper price from customers, even if sales are imperiled for a short period.

Finally, the conflict between short- and long-term thinking affects packaging. Temporarily fashionable packaging often is a sin against long-term brand-name marketing (where a long-term approach is required). Here the consequences of opportunism become obvious, because fashionable short-term behavior eventually destroys consumer confidence. Ultimately this leads to loss of respect for that product, brand, and company.

Encouraging competitive advantage through innovation and research and development is absolutely necessary, for it is a part of the dynamic structure of a free-market economy. Nestlé feels that innovations must be tailored primarily to long-term consumer trends and desires. However, as marketers, companies should remember that innovation is not the only thing. Many innovations do not come directly from the market but rather from technological work or from research and development. Such innovations are created by researchers who invent new products that marketers have probably never—and customers *certainly* never—imagined. Of course, innovation must be followed by the most important phase of the investigation: seeing whether the new product makes sense to consumers.

There is a lot of talk about life cycles in marketing, in connection with innovations and product development. This is one of those nice marketing buzzwords that I mistrust. Examining a product's life cycle may lead to a fatalistic attitude, since, depending on the point in the cycle, mechanistic forecasts may actually bring about the downfall of a product.

To counteract such marketing theories, companies must maintain an optimistic outlook. There are thousands of ways to give existing products a new push by means of new ideas and minor changes. Since a revolutionary discovery cannot be made every day, renovation is as important a component of commercial success as any so-called great innovation.

In this context, I would like to add a provocative remark about "me too" or copycat products. I know that marketers, as a rule, despise them, but I want to put in a good word, just once, for "me too" products. First, because they are sensible from the free-market point of view; they increase competition, which stimulates the economy. Second, because every company has original products that have become almost marketing-taboo: no one thinks about them any longer, even though they should have been changed long ago. Then a clever "me too" producer changes the product slightly, differentiates it, and sells it cheaper. He may do very well in marketing his "me too" product against the original one. In my opinion this is the type of "creative imitation" that can lead to success, depending on the situation.

No company can engage in marketing at the expense of profits. The purpose of marketing, as everyone should know, is to increase profits. Yet too often this is misunderstood. Cost competition takes on greater importance in a tough, stagnating market. Taking a marketer's point of view, executives argue about the best solutions for the market, the smartest advertising ideas, and so forth. However, if marketing is not in line with costs, a company eventually will lose out to the competition in the area of costs.

Keeping pace with competitors' costs plays a major role in any company's strategic considerations. It is a prerequisite for Nestlé's ability to maintain a price policy that will keep us in the market while simultaneously yielding a profit. There are numerous approaches here, and I'm not thinking of production costs alone. Those can be reduced by improving manufacturing methods, by planning and discipline, and by faster machinery. Taking a marketer's point of view, I sometimes talk about "cost-efficient sales": sloppy marketing, unduly small orders or customer base, and inappropriate products can put an excessive burden on a company's entire cost structure. Segmentation and giving in to the market have to stop somewhere. Faced with such a scenario, a company has to consider carefully whether it would not be better to abandon the segment and to handle other products at lower costs.

There are also important cost aspects to advertising. Nestlé's marketing teams are always asking senior management to increase the advertising budget, because competition is getting tougher. I remember David Ogilvy saying once that the difference between good and bad advertising, at identical costs, was 17 to 1 in terms of effectiveness. I can't prove that as accurately as Ogilvy, of course, but there does seem to be some truth to it, when one considers how much bad advertising there is out there.

I tell Nestlé's advertising staff that before I will agree to invest more money, they must first try to improve our advertising. The trick is to achieve greater continuity, not to start something new every day. It is just when a company is getting bored stiff with its advertising that that advertising is beginning to have an effect on consumers. Companies have to develop a feel for increasing the effectiveness of their advertising by improving its quality. Yet this is an aspect of marketing that appears to be too elusive for many marketers to grasp.

This brings us to the problem of individual brands and group brands. If budgeting is left to junior product managers and advertising agencies, naturally they will come up with a separate brand for each individual package, in order to obtain a gigantic budget from the company. A company can indeed push a product by this means—and be left with no profits. As entrepreneurs guided, not the least, by cost considerations, we should continue to argue for the economy of group brands and the usefulness of corporate brands, with reasonable differentiation for individual profiles. Even companies like Procter & Gamble and Unilever are returning to these concepts, for, in cases of extreme segmentation, sales of individual products are languishing below the profitability level, particularly given the density of all that advertising out there, which increases the cost of conveying an advertising message effectively.

Corporate image and its optimum use also belong in this complex of problems, along with marketing costs. For example, I myself have once again placed the name "Nestlé" more in the forefront at our company. Some of Nestlé's subsidiaries in faraway countries were named "Food Processing Ltd." or something of the kind. Now they are all named "Nestlé" again—and are proud of it.

Many short-term fashion trends are mistakenly referred to as "consumer trends." When talking about trends, it is important to distinguish between what the consumer really thinks and the current banter in pseudointellectual marketing circles. Naturally, Nestlé's young marketing people are impressed by a great number of "modern" trends; for example, there is "social" marketing, which might mean a message on every package stating that 2 cents of the price goes to "save the rain forest," or "environmental" marketing, where the message generally reads: "This can is recyclable." Some of this makes sense, of course, and these trends have penetrated people's consciousness. Under normal circumstances, however, charity and social obligations should not be confused with corporate marketing—which is why I feel that some limits are necessary.

Marketing staffs propose such marketing and advertising measures because they themselves have gradually become infatuated with these ideas, and so they keep looking for ways to use company money to propagate their convictions. There are quite a few marketing experts in the advertising business who doubt whether any advertising can be justified. They say companies should only provide product information; everything else, according to them, is wrong. However, consumers are reached primarily on an emotional level; and as long as advertising remains permissible, companies must speak to consumers' emotions too. At the very least businesses should determine objectively to what degree informative—as opposed to emotional—advertising contributes to the sale of a product.

On the other hand, Nestlé often receives so-called creative suggestions or presentations from advertising agencies. Upon careful examination they usually turn out to consist merely of cheap gags, which do nothing at all for the product. So companies must constantly be on their guard to ensure that they do not succumb to one trend or the other.

I'd like to add something a bit provocative about a particular trend in the food industry. In my opinion, "nutrition" is being overemphasized. The nutritional and physiological aspects of food are essential, of course, given the critical contribution a good diet makes to health and well-being. However, food has another purpose as well: people want to fill their stomachs as pleasantly as possible with food that tastes good and is easy to digest. We must never forget that basic fact.

For instance, for years now people have been running chocolate down. And this despite the facts that (a) negative ideas about the amount of calories and sugar it contains are completely wrong, and (b) chocolate is a taste preference, a perennial favorite of consumers. Chocolate consumption in Europe has increased every single year. In spite of all the talk about health, therefore, food companies should not let themselves be blinded to what consumers really want.

We have all learned that marketing is not omnipotent. In the 1960s, marketers (myself included) believed that consumers bought a product exclusively because of our marketing campaigns. When the market became more difficult, we found to our astonishment that consumers never buy a product just because of marketing—they also simply want something worthwhile for their money. In our free-market society, consumers have freedom of choice, which is why some things never happen the way we marketing people think they should.

Some examples. The German car manufacturer Opel has a lightning bolt in its logo and a car called the Rekord (as in *record-break-*

ing)—yet no consumer has ever confused the Rekord with a Porsche. Or take the case of France. Everyone knows that the French do not hate France; nevertheless, 50 percent of the cars the French buy are made outside of France. This is clear evidence that consumers decide on the basis of their own needs and not according to any general opinion they may have of a company or a certain mode of behavior.

This independence on the part of consumers provides companies with an opportunity. Nestlé has been subjected to boycotts based on politically motivated criticism. In practice, however, they have had hardly any effect at all on company sales, because in the final analysis consumers decide for themselves what they really want to buy, and are well able to separate political discussions from their own personal interests.

Another new trend that has its pitfalls is the craze for "personalized" products. Nestlé, too, has joined this crowd, introducing a chocolate bar in the United Kingdom and America no longer merely called "Nestlé" but "Henry Nestlé." Germany has a famous brand of beer called "Henninger" that is now being sold as "Christian Henninger."

This strategy may be successful. I do feel, however, that we executives must keep a careful eye on marketing ideas that are suddenly in vogue, to see whether we are dealing with a short-term notion or with a concept that will produce long-term results. We should not overestimate or exaggerate any individual aspect of marketing.

The same caution applies to the retail trade. Here too we are dealing with different concepts such as supermarkets, discount stores, and many other retail concepts. Mistakes are frequent. For instance, it is just not possible to upgrade any old supermarket to a higher price category simply by claiming that its concept is "fresh." The facility, its location, customer segment, operating concepts, and all the rest must be coherent.

With all the current specialization in marketing, people tend to forget that every aspect must fit into an integrated whole. Otherwise they will find themselves wondering why a good idea for a certain segment ruined their whole program. Attacks on marketing are certainly part of the marketing trend. I am referring to "consumerism," not as a genuine representation of consumer interests but as an ideology in which everything from advertisements to corporate policy comes under attack. Those who advocate these ideas are often people who fight to give citizens and consumers greater responsibility on the political level. Clearly, however, those same people do not believe that citizens are capable of making their own daily decisions, as consumers, without being led by the hand by government agencies and legislation.

It goes without saying that consumers need to be protected to make sure that no harmful additives are included in a product, that the label is correct, and that they are provided with proper information. However, we must not forget that there is a cost/benefit ratio in this area too. Citizens should ask whether the enormous costs of "consumerism" are commensurate with real benefits to consumers. If the cost/benefit ratio is distorted, proponents of "consumerism" will lack the credibility needed to influence today's consumers.

One final comment on the exaggerations so frequent in marketing: They often produce the opposite of what a company wants, and undermine its credibility. The ironic old Arab saying, "Everyone calls his own lice gazelles," expresses this very nicely.

MARKETING MEANS SELLING

Many young people working in marketing are the exact opposite of what companies really need in that field. The reason such people want to be in marketing is not because they can truly say, "Selling Nescafé fascinates me; that's the whole purpose of my life." Neither can they say that they would like to help the company develop or sell its products, or something of the kind.

Like others in their circle, they just consider marketing very chic. Their only concern is to impress their social set by saying that they are product managers or market researchers. They want to impress people, optimize their self-satisfaction, and be promoted. Such people never stop to think about how they might sell products, solve problems, or help a business to move forward.

There are, on the other hand, a great number of people who really do want to help when they join a company. Top managers should carefully consider which people to take on and who is right for which position. There is no better sales argument than the salesman's personal conviction about his message, because "no one who is convinced himself has trouble convincing other people." That is the secret of being persuasive. It also means that marketers must use company products in their homes—a directive that executives will have to repeat over and over again.

Another problem should be mentioned here: marketing people can be too far removed from real consumers. Sometimes they miss things by virtue of their upbringing and education. This problem is less prevalent in Switzerland, because people live closer together and so are confronted with the same everyday realities. However, in the larger markets, marketers often are so far removed from real consumers that market research is the only means of determining consumer wants and needs. Personal communication with consumers becomes impossible, except through advertising in the media.

Television commercials are the right thing for a mass market, but it is advantageous to a company for marketers to maintain personal contacts with consumers as well. This applies both to information and to communication. Market research is important in an anonymous market, and an essential foundation for sound marketing, but it can't replace the knack that the best marketing experts have for understanding consumer behavior.

In a society with a market economy, presidents of consumer-oriented companies must also be the top salespersons. They must put themselves at the head of all their sales personnel. This doesn't mean they have to sell, in the strict sense of the term, but rather that they must radiate the spirit and mentality of a leading salesperson throughout the company. For a while now, selling has taken a backseat to new marketing techniques. As times become more difficult, all executives should rediscover the value of being a true salesperson and learn to appreciate his/her function and usefulness once again.

Of course, much has changed in sales as well. Modern salespeople need more knowledge, as they now sell systems and/or solutions. More demands are made on them, as they talk to people in the trade who are trained managers with practical experience. Because of all this, salespeople should also participate in the formulation of marketing plans and strategy. Through their work in the field, salespeople hear a great deal that it would be well to include in marketing plans. Nonetheless, the sales mentality and sales attitude itself should not change. The Chinese have a saying: "A person who cannot smile should not open a store." This will be true for as long as someone tries to sell something to someone else.

4

Protecting Brands and Promoting Sales

H ere are six of the basic principles of advertising at Nestlé:

1. Preserving continuity in advertising over a long period of time, coupled with the cumulative effect of such advertising, is just as crucial and important as having advertising of high quality. In addition to continuity in advertising, continuity among the people who deal with advertising and in promoting brands often plays a role.

2. The need for continuity, together with the importance of advertising and its high cost, are the reasons why I feel so strongly that advertising is a management task and cannot be delegated to junior brand managers and advertising agencies' customer-contact people, who change continually.

3. Of course, if these advertising tasks and decisions about advertising are to be shifted more and more to a committee of top executives, those executives must understand something about advertising. This is something to take into account when choosing managers, and it implies a need to provide training in advertising. It also means that the managers concerned should not only give their opinions and their thumbs-up or thumbs-down at the final presentation, but also participate in setting marketing and advertising goals from the start and during briefings. This is the only way to avoid eleventh-hour remarks like, "That yellow needs a touch of blue."

4. Just a word about media planning: It is much more than arithmetical calculations of net customer reach and contact costs, with a bit of sociodemographic data thrown in.

5. With all due respect for purely aesthetic advertising, companies should not forget *information*, even though information isn't

everything in advertising. Like any other long-term strategy, advertising must be informed by a single, *reliable* message.

6. It is the job of advertising to promote current sales, to update offers, to support sales campaigns in the media, and to increase the potential for both future sales and short-term actual sales. Long-term advertising messages also can be updated with current features (e.g., price fluctuations, seasonal situations) in order to promote current sales.

Apart from quality and trademarks, advertising is the most important factor in building up and looking after brands. Remember that the basic purposes of advertising are to

1. Publicize a product or product information;
2. Build up a brand image;
3. Trigger the purchase of the product.

The more long-term advertising has publicized a product and given it a profile in advance, the easier the last function of marketing (triggering the purchase of the product) becomes.

The wonderful things about advertising—at once so full of opportunities and so terribly problematic, especially when one considers the huge amounts of money spent on advertising—are (a) the very big difference between good and bad advertising, and (b) the limited likelihood, despite market research, that we will discover exactly what kind we are paying for before we spend money on it.

I don't mean to imply that good advertising is always purely aesthetic advertising. Companies do, of course, want consumers to march to the tune of their advertising. (In ancient Greece, when Aeschines finished speaking, people said, "He spoke well," but after Demosthenes had roused them, they cried, "Let us march [against Philip of Macedon's army]!") When it comes to advertising, companies would do well to keep in mind Lao-tse's adage: "It is better to do nothing than to waste a lot of effort creating nothing."

Looking after brands and the whole communications policy needs to be included to a greater extent in the tasks and responsibilities of heads of individual operations, so that there are more uniform plans for advertising and trademark policy and so that they do not vary every time a marketing manager changes jobs. This is the way to achieve greater continuity and higher quality, and to have advertising better reflect corporate policy.

Briefings by advertising agencies should no longer be allowed without the approval of heads of individual operations, who should be present at all important presentations in the future. The interaction resulting from direct contacts between the heads of individual operations and the staff working on advertising and sales will automatically produce higher quality and greater continuity.

Here is a summary of some of the provisions of the advertising policy applied at Nestlé:

1. Put responsibility for media advertising at a high level in the company; the boss has to oversee advertising and brands.

2. Continually improve advertising quality and maintain continuity in advertising with a view to the long run.

3. Adapt advertising to specific media: use specialized media; make more use of fringe media; continue to increase efficiency (also through your own market research).

4. Include the most important technical trademark and advertising elements in all measures (display material, PR measures, etc.).

5. Adapt to new means of communication as early as possible. Goals for advertising and marketing should be compatible.

6. Advertising, sales promotion, and public relations should work together.

7. Reinforce regional advertising and regional focus on improving market share.

8. Use additional profits for media advertising, to reinforce brands and to benefit new products.

9. Constantly check the performance and the quality of the creative output of advertising agencies.

A pointer about advertising in trade journals: advertisements aimed at retailers often are neglected or not properly appreciated by manufacturers. However, they are an important instrument in the chain of communications with the trade. The more regional marketing becomes, the more companies need to take retail groups into consideration. The more the number of sales reps is cut, the more important it becomes to use such ads as a means of channeling real messages about products to the trade.

It is also important to build up long-term standing with the trade. The diverse output of a manufacturer does a good deal of that naturally. And there is also the sales apparatus. Here too I see a role for advertising in trade journals. For one thing, it reaches not just buyers in the trade but also the other employees in distribution and sales, who take part in decisions and often are badly informed about what a manufacturer has to offer or the background behind his offers. I often ask myself why this must be so.

Do our salespeople present their information and sales pitches so badly, or do the buyers in the trade neglect to pass on information to their own sales groups? I consider trade advertisements to be an extension of our salespeople, present everywhere that an actual salesperson no longer calls, because of withdrawal of customer coverage, or where he or she is no longer allowed to call because of some conditions in the trade. Finally, advertisements provide striking information. Moreover, in a survey by the GfK (German "Society for Consumer Research") of sources of information for retail food outlets, trade journals and sales reps tied for first place with approximately 80 percent.

Attacks on advertising by people whom one can take seriously are fueled by fears of being manipulated by advertising, which people want to avoid, and by certain forms of advertising that people feel are unreliable or unreasonable. In this context, I can remember German schoolbooks talking about advertising in quite a derogatory manner. I am convinced that, in their own self-interest and as professional communicators, advertising experts in particular should take it upon themselves to increase public awareness of two truths:

1. *Advertising is an integral part of a free-market economy.* Everyone with something to sell must have the right to tout their wares. Advertising provides information and an overall view of the market. Advertising costs as a percentage of sales are overestimated as a rule, and usually are more than compensated for by the effects of quantity rebates.

Advertising increases competition that is good for the consumer. Its power to manipulate people is quite simply exaggerated, as proven by many examples of consumer behavior. In our free-market economy, no consumer can be forced to buy a certain product. He or she has enough alternatives to choose from. The term "consumer terror" not only is objectively wrong, it also inadmissibly belittles real terror.

2. *Laws and present self-regulation by the industry ensure that advertising is honest.* The public is not as aware as it should be of that fact, nor does it realize to what extent the economy itself acts to regulate advertising.

I have already mentioned the enthusiasm and commitment that are needed in marketing. Here too, in connection with good advertising, I am reminded of the saying, "No one who is convinced has difficulty convincing other people." We must be persuasive rather than merely manufacture cheap gags. That is the only way to engage in successful advertising over the long run.

Sales promotion is primarily a tactical, not a strategic tool. Sales promotion should, once again, be more closely integrated into the overall advertising message on a product, on the one hand, and, on the other, into the goals, situation, and plans of the trade, or of specific retail groups and stores. Here there are areas of conflict between the trade and industry, of course. The conflict could certainly be reduced to a great extent, if industry would stop mounting national "steamroller" campaigns to promote sales.

Special discount prices should not be just a means of promoting sales; they also should be used (a) to reward the trade for its efforts to sell the products, and (b) as a part of price negotiations. Discounts that are too high or too permanent exaggerate price distortions, which necessarily have a negative effect on consumers in the end because they are confusing.

In spite of differing goals and the fact that the trade's activities are designed, first of all, to achieve its own marketing goals, industry and the trade have reasons for acting together. However, if industry does not want its sales promotion campaigns to end their life on the buyer's desk, it must keep a series of requirements in mind.

Because the trade makes its plans long in advance, industry and the trade need to come to an early agreement. Industry's means of promoting sales forms a part of the trade's overall advertising policy, which is why there needs to be timely agreement with stores or the headquarters of retail groups. That way, the promotion campaigns can be incorporated into their annual planning.

Spontaneity when coordinating industry's sales-promotion campaigns with the headquarters of retail groups is being replaced, more and more, by exact analyses and calculations of the advantages of one brand, or one group of goods, over another.

Industry's sales promotion must support the trade's goals in advertising as exclusively as possible. The more exclusiveness the supplier can promise the trade, the better the conditions for their common action. A sales-promotion campaign by industry that becomes a part of a storewide thematic promotion by the trade and, as a result, appears in all the media, can only satisfy the trade's interest in profiling if it is not being carried out in any other stores at the same time.

Such promotions will contribute all the more to profiling a store, the more the promotion enables it to give its customers specific advantages compared to its competitors. The limit, beyond which such collaboration with a retail partner becomes too intensive, is reached when it violates the principle that says that all customers are to be treated identically. And so, despite the differing interests of industry and the trade, it obviously is wise to coordinate sales-promotion policies.

When promoting sales, one should sell not just with discounts but also with constructive sales promotions. Remember the following:

- ☐ The special offer must emphasize the advertising theme at the point of sale.
- ☐ It must contribute to increasing consumption or to gaining new customers.
- ☐ The promotion must be accompanied by measures to support customers.
- ☐ It should offer customers practical solutions to their problems, and enable them to integrate the product into their lifestyles.
- ☐ In place of the former "steamroller" promotions, promotions now should be developed for a single retail group and its customers.

☐ When preparing a tailor-made promotion, keep in mind not only consumers but also the markets composed of two-stage businesses and wholesalers. They must receive enough supplies to be able to place products sensibly.

In order to make its policy as market leader more credible, Nestlé's policy is to reduce marketing discounts. Nestlé must try to simplify and improve the price structure in this way, so that the difference between the normal delivery price and the net price after deducting terms once again will become smaller. The net price must be an equitable one for the market, and the price must be honest.

Companies need to check their terms constantly, and to pay close attention, above all, to the following:

☐ Tighter control, and increased emphasis on profits for terms of sale;

☐ Adapting terms to the structure of the market;

☐ Distinguishing between those basic terms based on orders or on annual sales, as well as between terms and special discount prices;

☐ A tendency to reduce special discounts and to link them to the performance of the special offers, while taking the customs of the branch into account (performance, not tricks!);

☐ Setting the size of minimal orders in order to drop uneconomical business, and combining this with aggregate terms for wholesalers. In short, and to be explicit, I prefer *firms in better condition* to *better conditions of sale.*

5

All Business Is Local

One hears a lot of talk today about "global" marketing; it is the new buzzword, one that somehow also means "average" marketing. True, a development has taken place that makes marketing on a broader scale necessary. We now have satellite communication, larger markets, population shifts, and products that are sold worldwide in the same forms (gasoline, computers, etc.). In the food business, however, products are sold directly to consumers, and consumers greatly vary from country to country.

Consumer mentalities and eating habits in individual countries are so different that they prove that "all business is local." One might indulge in the rather malicious suspicion that "global" marketing was invented by headquarters personnel, looking for an opportunity to increase their power. But is that true?

Initially, marketing takes place in individual countries and in individual markets. The consumers are there, and so are the specific circumstances, habits, and mentalities to which companies must adapt. Of course, it isn't wrong to have a number of international strategies and theories. Experiences can be exchanged. In brand policy and packaging design especially, it is not advisable to do something different in every country. For certain products, there are advertising experiences and principles that work almost everywhere.

It often makes more sense to work with an international agency, for a company can benefit from its multifaceted experience. Because of advertising overflow, satellite advertising, and similar factors, every company should accept expert advice on which aspects of local marketing or global coordination they need to emphasize.

If you work, as I do, at international headquarters, you should display some resistance to global marketing, on behalf of consumers. Since global marketing too often results in average ads that are slightly off the mark in every country, one ends up with a global competitive disadvantage.

In marketing, as in everything else, the future is hard to see. Looking at predictions of only 20 years ago and comparing them with today's realities should remind us of how careful we have to be with our forecasts for the future. What did we know or imagine back then about the collapse of Communism, the central importance of environmental issues, or the opening of the hole in the ozone layer?

Extrapolations aren't always as useful as we might think. Can they be replaced by creative imagination and vision? As I see it, intuition, information, and scientific marketing flow together. In the final analysis, intuition is *the creative use of information.*

Naturally, many trends can be perceived. A lot is known about population growth, medical progress, and so forth. I personally am convinced that, within 10 or 20 years, many environmental issues will have been solved. Yet there are many things, such as integrated communication systems, that remain difficult to grasp, although we have all read a great deal about them.

In the future the media mix will become more differentiated, presenting new opportunities to market a *targeted* message (as opposed to "the shotgun approach"). But most likely there will be additional restrictions on advertising. Attacks against advertising will increase, forcing companies to take a position on the issue.

Mass products will become even more indistinguishable in the future, but there will be a trend toward individualization and segmentation of consumption. The effects of more leisure time also will be seen. The trade's demand-driven power will reach its apogee and start to decline, resulting in a better balance between supply and demand and the creation of a more realistic atmosphere.

The consumer goods industry will be better able to balance price differentials between private and national brands, based on brand preferences and differences in quality acceptable to consumers. Companies will learn to charge less for products that are not distinctive.

Of course, the future of our sociopolitical system is crucial to marketing, because there could be no such thing as marketing without a market economy. I see fewer problems in this area, because we have excellent arguments to use against our critics. The collapse of planned economies over the past several years has shown that only a free-market economy satisfies consumer demand.

Problems may arise in connection with fundamentalism and purism. These phenomena encourage people to ignore reality and lock them into a priori systems. We have to remind our young people that there is no ideal world, no Utopia, that every system has its advantages and disadvantages. Otherwise they will turn every system upside down just because it isn't perfect.

In my opinion it is important for companies to pay less attention to forecasts and extrapolations, and to strive to foster a greater amount of creative imagination—an attitude, a willingness, and a mentality that are open to developments in the world. Companies must make it an important goal to stay alert to the consequences of new developments and to take necessary steps or make decisions quickly.

THE WORLD HAS BECOME A VILLAGE

An explosion in the means of communication, with content that easily jumps over national and ideological borders, characterizes not only the developments we have seen in the second half of the twentieth century but also the future we face. If most totalitarian systems have collapsed, and ideologically isolated countries are finding it harder and harder to survive, it is in no small part due to developments in communications.

Communication also is responsible for enabling a global middle class to take shape. Over time, and despite all of its ethnic, linguistic, and cultural differences and the many current problems connected to them, it will develop common attitudes and values and a common way of life. That global middle class will exert on existing social and political conditions a strong pressure for the freedom to evolve personally, economically, and professionally.

On the international level, there is a growing readiness to collaborate more closely in all areas. Powerful economic areas are forming in Europe, in North and South America, and in Asia, and starting to form in Africa as well. Also associated with global communication is a tremendous increase in information and an acceleration of scientific and technological development. Ninety percent of all the scientists who have ever been active on Earth are living today. Every 10 or 15 years, the amount of technical literature that is published annually doubles. In 1880, a mere 2 percent of the active population in the United States was working in the fields of information, science, or education; by the year 2000, that figure will have risen to 66 percent. The English soldier and writer Barnabe Rich would have been even more astonished today than in 1613, when he wrote, "One of this century's ills is the surfeit of books; the world is so overcrowded with them that it is impossible to digest the jumble of useless things that are thought up every day and thrown out into the world."

Yet today we can draw upon almost unimaginable technical resources for processing information. With approximately one million logical components per cubic centimeter, today's semiconductor elements are almost as densely packed with logic as the human brain. The first transistors of 1960 were a million times less densely packed and less efficient. Handling information is increasingly becoming a matter for the markets.

The services that information uses, such as the mail and telephones, which traditionally have been government monopolies, are being privatized more and more. In my opinion that is a new component in the development of communications.

Now that communications already are global, trade and payments are becoming more global as well. World trade is growing faster than the GNP in individual countries. Globalization has progressed the furthest in foreign exchange transactions. At present, between $800 billion and $1 trillion are exchanged daily. Only 5 percent of that amount is for actual goods. At the world's five biggest stock exchanges, shares and bonds worth more than $2 trillion are exchanged annually.

Global communications, coupled with worldwide liberalization, open up tremendous opportunities for companies with operations all over the world. Cross-border industrial and financial operations, technology transfers, the spread of habits of consumption and of corporate management and communication within companies—all these make true global operations possible for the first time.

Global segments, global brands like Nescafé, Coca-Cola, Mercedes Benz, and certain whiskey and cosmetic brands, spread throughout the world much faster and more extensively by modern means of communications.

Regional habits also spread throughout the world, thanks to modern marketing and modern communications. Look at Italian and oriental cooking, English furniture or golf—all tastes that once were local but now have spread worldwide. Although there is no one generalized trend in consumption worldwide, there are various segments of consumption, or lifestyles, that are spreading throughout the world, so there are still local segments.

Here, in conjunction with modern means of communication, companies like Nestlé can, to a great extent, spread regional habits of consumption all over the world on a large scale. Local advertising increasingly can be supplemented by advertising with worldwide media delivered by satellites and television stations; by the creation of newspapers and magazines with worldwide circulation; and by the constantly increasing amount of travel. There are also many opportunities, often overlooked, for small and medium-sized companies.

Formerly, a small company was unable to operate all over the world. There was no global communications network, no fax machine. Today those obstacles no longer exist. Communication and information have to adapt to these new circumstances, become more professional, look for new means and ways of appealing to different target groups in accordance with their needs and characteristics, in part by making use of various media.

Company heads also spend more time now on information and information policy. Nowadays the ability to communicate is an important part of the ability to manage: talking; informing and explaining; motivating and convincing people inside and outside the company; interviews; discussions; personal contacts (including those with critical groups)—all these belong to the daily life of today's businessperson.

Transparency and openness are the best business policy in the long run, and the development of modern communications has had a lot to do with the transparency in business and capitalism today. Kant's categorical imperative could be modified to apply to communication policy: "Run your company so that everything you do is fit to be published in tomorrow's paper."

Global communications also are the reason why an event at Nestlé's subsidiary in Chile or Thailand—especially if it isn't a good one—becomes known all over the world in a matter of seconds. Any problem anywhere becomes the whole world's problem. That helps to define our firm's policy in individual countries as well as Nestlé's internal and external policy on information.

With regard to the effectiveness of communications flowing from top management, we executives are faced with a dilemma—especially when we manage a company we don't own. Communication works best when it is personal; that is the best transmission belt. But executives realize that personality cults are wrong. The company, and not the person giving the message, should profit from the communication and be able to create an image for itself. Company heads come and go; therefore, each of us should consider him- or herself as merely a link in a chain, and act accordingly.

Global communications also make greater demands on companies to develop clear corporate strategies and an understandable corporate policy, and to pay closer attention to everything that is conveyed by corporate image, corporate identity, and corporate culture today. This presents something of a problem for a worldwide, decentralized company like Nestlé. On the one hand, Nestlé has to stress a uniform policy, and cohesion; on the other hand, a part of that policy is to integrate the traditions and consumption habits of individual countries into its policy as far as possible. This is why part of Nestlé's image and corporate structure is different in every country, or even in every product category.

As a result, even global marketing (that buzzword of our times) has limits, at least for a company in the food industry like Nestlé. Take habits of consumption, for example. Consumer habits and the structure of the clientele are very variable in our branch; this makes it necessary to vary policies. Legislation and market share also are variable and, again, require different strategies. Nor can advertising be totally globalized: it's still difficult to sell to Germans using advertising heavy in English humor.

The obtaining of funds, money markets, and investors all are important elements in today's global competition, in connection with the globalizing of communications. Price/benefit ratios play a big role, as do optimization, shareholder value (a new buzzword), credit potential, and the various opportunities to increase equity. Increasingly it is becoming clear that all of these are important factors in international competitiveness.

Nestlé is a company that sells to the whole market: We want to reach consumers, customers, all over the world. It is right for money markets to be as open as our international, liberal collaboration. Therefore it is logical that, in keeping with its international outlook,

Nestlé uses money markets all over the world, with the result that its sources of capital correspond more and more to the geographic distribution of its activities throughout the world.

New methods of operational management of a multinational company, using today's means of communication, contribute to much better planning and more efficient tools for steering internal processes and procedures. For instance, within one European association production is programmed so that a company knows what is being produced every second in a particular country and sold in another. As a result, it can harmonize its production programs. There is also, of course, a danger in this, particularly for headquarters.

The potential for headquarters to be on-line with Korea or Argentina brings with it the danger of centralization, for every manager automatically feels that he or she has to be in daily contact with those places to determine what is going on there. I have to some extent forbidden our computers to be programmed in such a way as to make that possible, just in order to prevent this new aspect of continuous control that can reduce flexibility, commitment, and identification with the market.

Let's face it, there's just too much information out there nowadays. What is being put out is, in part, merely "art for art's sake." The problem for executives like us, on the upper floors of management, is to judge it all properly. On the one hand, we have experts to organize the whole world of computers for us. On the other, we have managers who know better than we do what they really need, and we often build rather faulty bridges between these two different interests. It is important to have people in between, people both with experience in management and with a basic understanding of that "other world"; this prevents the paper jungle from becoming boundless, while ensuring that what must be done and utilized *is* done and utilized.

Furthermore, despite all the modern means of communication, I believe that travel still is necessary. The technicality of all that information and communication calls for a counterweight in the form of personal contacts. That is why, at Nestlé, a personalized style of management is considered a very important way of avoiding the gigantism and anonymity of big corporations. I myself am away from my office, traveling, more than half the time. My trips provide information, enable me to judge our managers and to motivate staff. I can give an impetus to operations on-site, and make decisions. There is an old saying: "Under the eye of the owner, meadows become fertile."

The development of the information society and global communications often brings with it a surfeit of information. This is also true of specialized aspects of communication, namely advertising. Every American adult is bombarded by 3000 ads every day, or as someone recently put it, "Nowadays, we live in a period of word inflation and thought recession."

The result of worldwide communications, coupled with worldwide liberalization and the formation of common markets, is more competition. Therefore, performance will be rewarded even more in the future than it has been in the past, and mistakes will be penalized even more severely. This applies both to countries and to companies.

Countries will find themselves facing much stronger rivalry for competitive advantage. Within common markets, the advantage of being big will no longer be as marked as previously, when markets were just opening up. Today, a small country once again has the opportunity of being chosen as the site of production facilities for a large economic area, if the on-site conditions are good, because markets now have opened up. In the past, in a protectionist phase, economies of scale could not be fully utilized in a small country, so plants had to be located in big countries. This has changed, which means it is no longer necessarily an advantage to live in a country with 80 million inhabitants.

The rapidly developing volume of communications and of communication techniques is, unfortunately, not entirely conducive to modern man's ability to communicate. True, knowledge of foreign languages is growing; but the culture of language, the precision of concepts, and the art of rhetoric all are declining. I don't think people understand each other any better now than they once did, or that they have a better grasp of the art of conversation than they used to, to say nothing of better-cultivated manners. On an international and global plane, however, communications certainly have led to greater mutual understanding.

As was true yesterday and will be true tomorrow, life is full of opportunities and risks; this applies to global communications as well.

In the end, the corporate attitude and abilities of each company will determine whether a company makes greater use of opportunities or is overwhelmed by risks and dangers, or at least adversely affected by them. The ancient Chinese were ahead of us in all this: the ideogram for *opportunity* in Chinese is the same as the one for *risk*.

6

Acquisitions as a Marketing Strategy

There are no universally applicable theories about the ideal strategies for marketing or acquisitions. There are "only" concrete solutions that vary from company to company and over time (i.e., adapt to new circumstances inside and outside the company). Though the following solutions primarily are Nestlé's, they should be of interest to other companies.

Today's Nestlé Corporation is the result of a combination of internal growth—due both to new products (Nescafé and Yes cakes are just two examples from among the many products launched by the Group) and to new markets gained by directly investing all over the world—and growth through takeovers and acquisitions. The history of Nestlé's development resembles the root system of a healthy tree: once the runner roots have been brought together, they continue to grow vigorously. The Nestlé Group has more than SFr. 50 billion ($35.5 billion) in annual sales at present—which makes it the world's biggest food company.

Nestlé is a worldwide company twice over: because of its size, and because of its orientation. (Less than 2 percent of Nestlé's sales stem from its native Switzerland.) Yet neither the size nor the international scope of Nestlé are ends in themselves, or matters of prestige—they simply result from the company's function.

Nestlé made a milestone acquisition very early in its history—in 1905—when it merged with the Anglo-Swiss Condensed Milk Company in Cham, Switzerland. The goal was stated in the merger agreement: "To utilize the experience both companies have gained in manufacturing and selling condensed milk, infant cereal, and similar products." To Nestlé's four factories in Switzerland and one each in Norway, Great Britain, Germany, Spain, and the United States, were added three more factories in Switzerland, four in Great Britain, and two in Norway. There was a new emphasis on an international model.

The mergers and acquisitions since then have been part of a long-term strategy; over time there has been a shift in emphasis, but not in basic concept.

During the 1960s and 1970s, the emphasis was on diversification. As refrigerated and frozen-food products began to stand out as two areas with a particularly high potential for growth, the Nestlé Group planned a traditional two-pronged strategy for entering those fields: development of new companies in areas that could make use of existing experience on a broad basis, and acquisitions in the product areas/markets in which Nestlé was looking for additional know-how, somewhat further away from what it had been concentrating on, in production, product design, distribution and sales policy, advertising and pricing. (Those acquisitions included, from 1962 to 1969, Findus International, a company that was active selling frozen foods primarily in Scandinavia and England at the time, and in 1973 the Stouffer Corporation in the U.S., also—but not just—a successful frozen-food company.) In order to diversify, several other takeovers were carried out parallel to, or shortly after, the acquisitions and investments in the expanding area of frozen foods.

FOUR PRINCIPLES OF ACQUISITION

Here are the four basic principles of Nestlé's acquisitions strategy:

1. *First principle.* A takeover is truly successful only if both parties carry it out in an atmosphere of willingness to learn from each other. Success in marketing depends primarily on a combination of employees' knowledge and their experience—if employees are not willing to transmit their knowledge or to use it, an important effect of synergy will fall by the wayside.

2. *Second principle.* A company's own strengths should be introduced into every acquisition. A decisive precondition is financial resources. We had turned to strengthening the Group's resources beginning in 1980-81, before Nestlé's series of important takeovers of the mid-1980s got under way. What is more, the liquidity available to

finance takeovers is only a partial, and not even necessarily the most important, aspect.

Naturally, it is agreeable and often also advantageous if an acquisition can be completely, or for the most part, immediately financed using the company's own funds. However, in a country with a system of credit that functions well, it would be absurd for entrepreneurs not to be prepared to take temporary advantage of outside funds. It was more important to Nestlé, in that phase, to strengthen the Group's profitability permanently. In the period between 1980 and 1987, Nestlé increased its return on sales from 2.8 to 5.2 percent—i.e., almost doubled it.

Another element that needs strengthening involves structures, range of products, and market position. Nestlé's takeover of Rowntree was successful mainly because the Nestlé Group had proved (with the Yes cakes and other products) that it was well able to launch and hold a position in the market segment of the company it was taking over.

3. *Third principle.* The Nestlé Group is not interested in taking over companies that are having economic difficulties. Our motto is, "The Group not only offers strength, it is also looking for strength." Decisive factors in our decisions are, for instance, the long-term growth potential of a company, its marketing know-how, and its technology.

4. *Fourth principle.* Nestlé restricts new acquisitions to areas that—either from the market and/or production processes—can be linked to its range of existing and newly acquired product range and linked to already existing or newly acquired experience. That means, on the one hand, refusing to become a conglomerate and, on the other, refusing vertical integration, production of raw materials, or retailing.

I repeat what I said at the start: These principles apply to Nestlé. They may be valuable as an example of a successful concept, but they cannot claim to be universally applicable. Other companies have successfully applied different concepts.

While Nestlé still follows these principles, our acquisition strategy has to some extent changed direction since the mid-1980s, through a change in emphasis. At present there is a strong tendency toward globalization of markets. In the area of capital goods, only the best machines have been good enough for many years now—and the best of these catch on quickly all over the world.

As far as globalization is concerned, recently the field of consumer goods has followed suit—electronic consumer goods are the clearest examples. Young people listen almost simultaneously to the same music in Europe, in the United States, in Latin America, and in Eastern Europe; they also dress alike. Eating habits, but not necessarily foods, are steadily becoming more international. Markets are becoming global.

A company attempting, on its own, to be successful throughout the world can no longer proceed in stages, as some companies once did: first they should work on the home market, and only afterward try to conquer successive export markets. What is needed now is full presence, with approximately the same focus and stress, in all three major regional markets in the world: Europe, North America, and the Pacific basin, with emphasis on Japan. A company that plans strategically and takes a long view will also focus its full attention on third world markets.

A precondition for success in important markets in industrialized countries is an ability to enter the market on the same scale as a standard competitor. The criteria are strict, for the markets have become physically narrow even as the globalization of markets and companies has widened the range of products offered in those markets. For instance, the number of products sold in supermarkets in the U.S. has risen from 13,000 in 1981 to 21,000 in 1991.

This is a worldwide phenomenon, and it means that as a rule there is room for, at the most, only two or perhaps three branded products for each product, in addition to the trade brand of the chain. As a result, only the market leader and the second or perhaps third in the market can achieve a broad presence in the market.

Nestlé has already gone very far along the road to globalization. The acquisition of Carnation in 1985 already brought us quite a way toward our goal of reinforcing our presence in the U.S. market, and did so without upsetting the balance between our various ranges of products. Almost incidentally, but not unconsciously, Nestlé entered the pet food business.

Our acquisition of Buitoni was not a question of global balance but more a matter of reinforcing specific focal points in Nestlé's global concept: Nestlé strengthened its position in the Italian and European markets.

An aside: In the oft-quoted program for domestic markets, there will be an expansion to some extent in the consumption of new, standardized products with no links to local eating traditions (I am thinking about the Yes cakes I already mentioned, chocolate bars like Nuts, or specialties like Smarties and After Eight mints). This is thanks to easier trade across borders, which lower costs and hence prices. However, for "traditional" high-quality food products (Nescafé, frozen and refrigerated products), reducing administrative obstacles will not lead to standardization or a leveling of quality: diversity will remain, tastes will still vary. Therefore, for a company to retain its position in today's (still) national markets, it will continue to be important, in the future, for it to satisfy the requirements described earlier.

IMPORTANCE OF THE EFFECTS OF SYNERGY

Another reason for Nestlé's acquisition of Buitoni was to strengthen emphasis on certain products by putting pasta right in the middle of the Nestlé Group's preoccupations, whereas formerly it had been seen mainly as an ingredient in ready-cooked meals as well as a means of strengthening the Group's focus on frozen foods (Davigel) and high-quality chocolates (Perugina).

Nestlé's intention to intensify its focus on products and to become market leader in specific areas was even more clearly apparent in the Rowntree takeover. Our decision was strongly influenced by circumstances: a sudden increase in share-purchasing by Nestlé's competitor Jakobs-Suchard triggered the change in our discussions with the chocolate and confectionery manufacturer in York, England, from talks about joint ventures to a quicker tactic. However, only the timing and type of action were influenced by circumstances; strategic aspects were decisive with respect to the content of that agreement and remain so for all others. With Rowntree's brands, Nestlé purchased market share in the growing segment of chocolate bars—chiefly in continental Europe, but also in many other areas where people still think highly of British habits of consumption.

Here's another thought: market share should influence the strategic decision to take a company over, but it should not be the single influencing factor. Costs should play an important role in the decision: if a company wants to become the market leader, it is not enough for it to count solely on the annual expansion of the market; on the contrary, it will have to displace competitors. This causes disproportionate costs for the "attacker" as well as for the "attacked," which often means unnecessary costs for the entire economy.

In such cases, acquisitions are the most efficient solution. Taking cooperative rather than unilaterally aggressive action is useful only when market leadership is not confused with having a monopoly, or standard presence in the market confused with controlling the market. More specifically, a company the size of Nestlé needs competition if it is to keep fit. For that reason the Nestlé Group neither strives to nor actually takes a dominating position in any market or product area.

Purchasing market share as part of a long-term marketing strategy makes sense, in my opinion, only if the company making the acquisition is sure it can effectively defend that market share.

Finally, what are the effects of a market-oriented acquisition strategy? Synergies are the first important effect—they justify inserting sound companies into a bigger organization. To simplify the full explanation radically, while such synergies in the area of production result from the combining and streamlining of similar processes, in the area of marketing it is the companies' different strengths that are enhanced by mutual enrichment. Companies such as Carnation, Buitoni, or Rowntree and their brands now benefit from the Nestlé Group's consistent, successful policy of globalization.

A second effect is a wider range of brands. Nestlé's policy of acquisition is not aimed solely at combining big companies, at taking over firms with billions of dollars of sales. A recent example of the acquisition of a small, highly specialized company by the Group is that of Pasta & Cheese, a U.S. manufacturer of fresh pasta. The Nestlé Group's worldwide marketing experience and real access to the market now stand behind that company's products.

One may well ask how the synergies from acquisitions and globalization can be harmonized with the differing requirements of regional markets and with variable regional tastes. The answer is that in the food industry, globalization does not mean that, sight-unseen, products are simplified for the international market or, even easier, forced unchanged onto the rest of the world by one country. On the contrary, there has been a globalization of product-linked concepts such as quality and quality assurance, and of solutions suggested by consumers.

Nestlé uses its experience to the same extent in every market. For instance, when selecting high-quality coffee beans for Nescafé, Nestlé employs nonintrusive means of refining and processing as well as of maintaining taste and flavors. Then, however, the mixture of the various sorts of coffee and the degree to which the beans are roasted are very carefully adapted to local tastes—the result being that Nescafé tastes different in every country and still meets the highest possible quality standards everywhere. Here too there is no leveling, even though markets are becoming global.

All in all, acquisitions have grown in importance as tools for marketing, because markets rapidly are becoming global and also because circumstances are changing—the key term being *regional integration* in Europe, North America, and, in the future, in the Pacific basin. This has led to an increase in the rhythm of the normal trend toward mergers and takeovers. In the United States in particular, but also in Australia, takeover experts unacquainted with the branch and oriented toward short-term speculative profits have often turned this faster rhythm into a downright hectic one.

Later on that hectic rhythm always flags, and it is the acquisitions that remain. They contribute to structural adaptations and to the rapid spread of innovation in the world's markets, and they are strategic marketing tools as well as a means of improving marketing.

7

Leadership in Action, or How to Steer a Battleship

Over the past few years, discussions about multinational corporations have become more objective. Gone are the days when executives of multinationals were loudly shouted down, with irrelevant remarks, at roundtable discussions. Sneering articles in the press, which saw every multinational as being, a priori, a devil it needed to combat, have grown scarcer too.

The advantages of a market economy and of foreign direct investment are being recognized once again. The bankruptcy of countries without a market economy has contributed to this, as has the more intensive dialogue among multinational companies, international organizations, and various pressure groups. Another result is more objectivity and an improved climate for discussions.

More and more, people are coming to realize that it is often necessary—even vital—for corporations to be multinational, in an era when competition is organized on a worldwide level, when technology evolves rapidly, when necessary research costs huge amounts and investments need to be big, when the communication network covers the entire world, and when the division of labor in the economy extends across borders.

MANAGEMENT PRINCIPLES OF A MULTINATIONAL

As a general principle, employees, people, and products are more important at Nestlé than systems. Systems and methods, while necessary and valuable in the running of a complex organization, should remain managerial and operational aids but should not become an end in themselves. It is a question of priorities. A strong orientation toward human beings, employees and executives, is a decisive, if not *the* decisive, component of long-term success.

For that reason, Nestlé's foremost concerns are (1) the training and the continued development of its employees (employee relations and qualifications), and (2) living up to its corporate social responsibilities (which is in the company's own long-term interest). A working atmosphere with close personal contacts, a direct management style, credible executives, contact with one another that transcends the borders of our native countries or operating units—all of these are important features of Nestlé's corporate culture. At Nestlé, these features are nurtured and kept alive and vibrant by our staff's continuing awareness of them, especially our executives'.

Nestlé's second important principle is its focus on its products. The ultimate justification of a company has to do with selling consumers products that appeal to them because of the products' high quality, convenience, variety, and price—products that can stand their ground even in the face of fierce competition.

Nestlé gives priority to the long view. Admittedly, this makes it necessary to maintain a satisfactory level of profits every year—which we strive to do. That puts the firm in a better position to think about, and to act on, long-term prospects. As is well known, longer-term considerations and actions are possible only when a company isn't constantly fighting for short-term survival. A clear distinguishing between *strategy* and *tactics* comes up in this context. Nestlé wants to win the war, not just the next battle. More long-term thinking also would defuse many of the conflicts and contentions among the various individual groups. This applies to employment conditions and relations with employees as well as to the conflicts and opposed interests of the trade and industry.

As a general rule, *decentralization* is not just a word at Nestlé; it is a basic principle we practice daily. Switzerland is home to Nestlé's Swiss subsidiary, its international headquarters, and the registered office of its holding company. Even so, we in Switzerland are far from regarding ourselves as the hub of the universe. This open-minded attitude creates more operating strength and flexibility, and it enables Nestlé to make decisions better attuned to specific situations in a given country. This type of policy also generates stronger motivation in Nestlé's executives and employees, and greater identification with Nestlé's business.

Having a decentralized organization makes it necessary to be more systematic in filling executive positions. This includes making significant investments in management training and in developing executives who are not only good, but who can be trusted.

Lenin said, "Trust is good, control is better," but I believe that company heads should continuously try to foster conditions that encourage trust and that we should express confidence in our people from the start. Or as Goethe put it, "If you treat people the way they are, you make them worse. However, if you treat people the way they could be, you make them better."

Of course, companies must make sure that executives use this freedom in a sensible way, and must remember that executives also need a clear understanding of the company's overall goals. This is why Nestlé makes sure that executives with decentralized responsibility can handle such a great degree of leeway. In addition to making important strategic and financial decisions, Nestlé's international headquarters in Switzerland also is responsible for general principles and for coordinating Nestlé's individual markets worldwide. Headquarters provides know-how, capability, and expertise in production, import and export, marketing and organization, especially when this know-how or such experts are not permanently available on-site. Headquarters also concerns itself with training those Nestlé executives who work abroad. And it provides initial investment financing and coordinates Nestlé's research units, which are also partially decentralized.

A FRIENDLY STYLE OF MANAGEMENT? YES, BUT . . .

Nestlé is in favor of as simple an organizational structure as possible, with fewer levels of management and broad sectors of responsibility. Nestlé tries to avoid bureaucratic excess (too many rules and procedures) and an overrating of the importance of the hierarchic structure (which remains a necessity). This, along with Nestlé's policy of maintaining personal contact with executives and employees, serves the purpose of preserving flexibility and enthusiasm for work within a big company.

Another important principle at Nestlé is the use of an open management style; it is combined, however (and this is extremely important), with a very clearly defined top management at every level. Nestlé has no use for a lack of accountability, or for the power struggles that occur when management is done by committee. I prefer a team *with a top* to a team *as the top*.

As everyone knows, when people talk about managing and reorganizing companies and making decisions, things have to start at the top. In this regard, discussions about the duties and responsibilities of the executive board and the board of directors take place at Nestlé's headquarters in Switzerland.

Swiss law provides for several possibilities: a business may be run by the chairman, by a chief executive officer, or by a chief operating officer or president. What is important in this context is to define responsibility clearly. This prevents success from having "too many fathers," or, in the case of failure, the scapegoat from always being the other person. No matter how duties and responsibilities are established internally, it seems to me that it is important for the entire board of directors to exercise overall control and for the board to take systematic action wherever necessary. This is particularly true of decisions regarding management, whoever is in charge of it.

A very important problem of constant concern at Nestlé is that of how uniform Nestlé's principles, policies, rules of conduct, and strategies should be, and to what extent they should differ depending on the country, subsidiary or region, branch or group of products. This question is of crucial importance to the success of a multinational; yet, often, too little attention is paid to it. In general, Nestlé tries to limit the uniformity of its policy to a requisite minimum. This minimum of uniformity is then systematically enforced, unless the person responsible for a given market can come up with some good reasons to justify a deviation from policy.

It goes without saying that Nestlé tries to achieve maximum uniformity with regard to systems and methods. However, local personnel policy, marketing, product characteristics in general, and all the issues relevant to consumers and local competition are largely established on-site. Here, Nestlé merely provides guidelines that are adapted regionally. Our general policy is, therefore, to adapt the company as far as possible to regional circumstances, mentalities, and situations. It is not Nestlé's policy to do a great amount of business domestically and have just a few satellite subsidiaries abroad. Nestlé wants to be an "insider" in every country, not an "outsider."

Everyone should know what kind of company Nestlé is and where Nestlé originates, what its basic philosophy is, and that it intends to preserve the good Swiss virtues of pragmatism, realism, and a positive work ethic. However, people also should realize that Nestlé is liberal and open to the world at large. It goes without saying that Nestlé has, and wants to maintain, an international management (not just in Switzerland but in as many markets as possible), while at the same time strongly fostering the development of local managers. I would like to stress in this connection that, by rotating their managers and experts, multinational companies make a contribution to tolerance and mutual understanding among countries, one that should not be underestimated.

Personnel policy is the key to all other matters. That is why the selection of the proper managers is so crucial. The higher the level of the executive, the more his overall personality (in addition to his intelligence, education, and experience) plays a role in how he handles his job. A candidate's character, sense of responsibility, and moral fiber are the primary things. Moreover, the following characteristics should in my opinion be prominent in any executive candidate:

- ☐ *Courage, solid nerves, and composure.*
- ☐ *Readiness to learn, sensitivity to new developments, and an ability to form an idea of the future—or "vision," as it is termed today.* To develop these qualities, a person must be well informed beyond the traditional management information system. Executives should take a lively interest in world affairs and make use of all conversations, contacts, and travel to satisfy their curiosity.
- ☐ *A capacity for both inner- and outer-directed communication and motivation.* Any executive unable to give clear information or to motivate and inspire people will have a hard time of it in this day and age.
- ☐ *The ability to create and sustain an atmosphere of innovation.*
- ☐ *The ability to think in context.*
- ☐ *Credibility; consistency in word and deed.*

In addition to that, I have often insisted on the necessity of having an international outlook and of being willing and ready to change.

Leadership qualities of the kind I have described are needed not only by top managers but in differing degrees by executives at all levels. At Nestlé, that means our roughly 10,000 managers out of a total of 200,000 employees.

In international markets, Nestlé trains local staff to assume responsibility, and also includes international executives on the management team. This brings more experience and variety to management, which is good for business.

Over the past 20 years there has been a lot of talk, most of it coming from the United States, about job rotation. To a certain extent, this does indeed serve to train and develop executives and to bring fresh ideas into management teams. Nonetheless, the importance of continuity in management should not be underestimated, nor should the value of that experience and knowledge that is acquired only when a specific task has been performed over and over again. Many companies have retained the same management team for years, or even for decades, because it has shown that it knows how to make the company perform successfully and grow dynamically.

To ensure strong management over the long term, a company should continually hire and develop trainees, especially in the larger markets. After 10 to 15 years, they will be ready for management assignments. It is important to Nestlé that one-third of such individuals be willing to take on international assignments. I also strongly believe in putting together a management team that is complementary, since no one person ever has *all* the requisite qualities and experience.

Nestlé does not want to become either a conglomerate or a portfolio manager. It wants to conduct only those businesses about which it has some special knowledge. Nestlé wants to be a global company, not a conglomerate hodgepodge. It regards acquisitions and efforts at diversification as a logical supplement to its business, but only in the context of a well-understood corporate and marketing policy.

A company needs to create and sustain a climate of innovation in connection with company growth. A reasonable amount of risk capital also must be made available. If heads of companies are not prepared for renewal, and do not take the initiative in planning and in making appropriate changes, then they are not entrepreneurs, not real doers, but mere do-nothings. On the other hand, managers should not continually be searching for big, dramatic innovations. Do not underestimate the importance of renovation and of constantly renewing and adapting your range of products. Exchanges of information on an international level also should be used to foster business.

I have some thoughts about a blanket organizational concept that is often discussed; that is, regionalization as opposed to the creation of product divisions. In general, the more homogeneous a business is, the more a regional concept should be preferred—with, of course, a few divisional elements. Exploring and coordinating product know-how and development to the maximum is, in the final analysis, not a line job. Furthermore, organizational charts also should be adapted to the strengths and experience of the people available.

Data processing and integrated computer networks provide a big, international company with many opportunities. However, the fact that one can be on-line every second with a subsidiary over 10,000 kilometers away should not be allowed to deflect a company from deliberate decentralization of operations and decision making.

A company that operates worldwide does need tools for planning and control. In the planning process, Nestlé needs "top-down" ideas and figures as well as "bottom-up" planning. In general, plans should contain far fewer figures and more goals and methods, as well as qualitative planning aspects.

Although, in large corporations, there may be acceleration in such areas as human behavior, technology, etc., such companies usually are battleships, not speedboats. They often cripple individual initiative and lose their ability to adapt quickly. Furthermore, the big corporation's pride and satisfaction over what has been achieved too often is at odds with the spirit of innovation. For this reason, one of top management's major tasks is to initiate change in good times, to inform and convince staff, to create a positive climate and a readiness inside the company to accept changes and new initiatives. Once again the Americans have coined a handy buzzword, *changemaster,* which they use to characterize a certain type of effective manager.

Let me also emphasize the importance of timing in the overall success of a corporation. A person who recognizes a development early and acts or makes the appropriate decisions, even if his idea is perhaps a little ahead of its time, will be more successful, simply because of that head start. Occasionally, however, it may happen that a certain idea or measure is developed before its time was ripe.

Change need not come in the form of big, dramatic innovations, or restructurings. It should be accepted as a continuous process, with constant adjustments in every area. However, care must be taken to remain true to fundamental corporate attitudes and goals. From a strictly organizational point of view, flexible, simple structures are best; excessively large units should be avoided wherever possible. In this respect, Nestlé has a natural advantage: Although it is a big company, it is spread out over many countries, and each of Nestlé's numerous factories has its own management and responsibilities.

The responsibility for accelerating needed changes rests primarily with top management. There are a number of possible techniques or modes of behavior here. I sometimes speak of "management by provocation," because certain provocative statements often provoke reactions and thoughts more rapidly and get processes moving quickly. To introduce change, top executives also need strength of character, authority, and credibility: What we say and do must be consistent. As far as I'm concerned, my personal contacts and conversations with Nestlé's managers and employees in individual countries are absolutely vital. Written guidelines or memos cannot replace them, which is why I spend half of my time traveling.

DIVERSITY IN PREFERENCE TO SIMPLICITY

When it comes to "concentrations in the economy," the crucial issue is not size itself but keeping competition alive. Today, competition often must be considered from an international point of view, because Europe, the United States, Japan, and a number of newly industrializing countries are all competing among themselves. Furthermore, the concepts of power and corporate size often are almost absurdly exaggerated, for a company's power is limited, in many cases, by legislation, competition, regulatory bodies, and publicity.

It is important not to exaggerate, or to conduct the debate about company size or about multinationals and small and medium-sized businesses on an ideological level. Apart from the requirements of competition, from a business point of view it is desirable for a firm to achieve the size best suited to a specific industry or mode of production. Considerable size is necessary if a company is to remain competitive on an international level, and if there is to be massive investment in research and technology. On the other hand there are many opportunities open to small and medium-sized companies, if they restrict themselves to special products or local activities, or to operating in the service sector. Diversity is what is important.

8

Managing and Motivating Employees

I t is right to expect the head of a company to be the chief motivator of its managers and employees. This means that he or she must measure success, provide guidelines, select managers more systematically, and audit management. My rule is to always and invariably keep to the long view: to win the war, not just a battle.

The long view also is needed in marketing and investments, and in personnel policy especially. Companies should consider the sums they devote to developing and fostering managers and to training employees so as to raise product quality, as being not merely costs but also investments in the future. The amount of money spent is not the only important thing; *how* it is spent is more important. There is no need to offer one's managers courses on the nature of the decision-making process or the psychological background of interaction, much less on Chinese ceramics. What companies must have in place is training aimed at working goals and requirements, using highly placed managers as teachers and discussion partners as often as possible.

More continuity and less fluctuation are the hallmarks of any realistic, long-term policy. This is why job rotation—necessary, and so popular today—always must be weighed against much-needed continuity in management. In the long run, managers need to take measures to inspire trust and to convince employees that we really *are* all in the same boat. The more both sides take a short-term view of matters, the more labor unrest inevitably grows.

As a general rule, the personnel manager is not the head of the staff but rather the manager of the personnel department. There is nothing worse than having heads of departments, divisions, or operating units who think that matters involving personnel are a problem for the personnel department. The personnel department has an important job to do, of course, in terms of daily personnel tasks and advising management, and it also must see to it that the basic principles of personnel policy and procedures are handled the same way throughout the entire company (unless circumstances in specific countries, or varying corporate structures, justify acting differently).

Pretentious phrases should not be used in the carrying out of personnel policies and tasks. This applies right off the bat to the designation given the personnel department, sometimes called the "human resources" department or something of the kind, and also to all those slogans that supposedly improve relations with employees: "cooperative management," "participatory management," etc. Of course, such designations and slogans usually have a kernel of truth in them and can place needed emphasis on important matters. But employees can always tell the employers who produce mere slogans from those who are honestly trying to execute their personnel tasks and therefore approach employee management with the right attitude.

Too often, true management is replaced by systems. We might even say: The less real management there is, the more the whole company is crammed full of personnel systems—systems to establish salaries, to measure merit; classification systems; detailed rules for managing employees; and on and on. This costs a lot of money and produces nothing. It destroys motivation and often steers the personnel department in the wrong direction. Concentration on personnel tasks that are really necessary and useful, as well as having bosses in place who are well aware of what those real tasks are, makes it possible to reduce sharply the size of the personnel department.

Important prerequisites for working efficiently in personnel and for motivating employees are

□ Broad areas of responsibility;
□ Few rungs on the management ladder;
□ Managers who are competent and who delegate responsibility.

Furthermore, corporate structures should be simple and comprehensible. Communications and information should not be arranged pyramidally. Finally, there should not be detailed job descriptions or definitions of authority; rather, management should see its task as one of resolving conflicts and implementing new policies.

Although at Nestlé we try to take the mentality and customs of individual countries into account, there are certain general principles that we apply everywhere:

- A positive attitude toward work,
- Pragmatism; realism,
- An open-minded approach to the world,
- A minimum amount of systems and written guidelines,
- A personal style of management,
- An atmosphere of mutual trust rather than of intrigue,
- No showing off; no windy rhetoric; no hypocritical remarks,
- No leaflets on corporate culture,
- A marked stress on practical experience and on the setting of good examples.

The most beautifully crafted personnel statements will remain useless if a company permits its managers to flout these principles simply because those managers are professionally good. Nestlé's slogans would be put down as merely so much hot air forever after. Of course, the shortcomings of individual employees have to be tolerated, but cardinal "sins against the Holy Spirit" must be sanctioned decisively. Corporate culture is a thing that must be built up over years and decades, and therefore it needs to be constantly cultivated by a responsible management team and carefully adapted to new circumstances now and then. It is something so subtle that it is hard to define. Somewhere I read that corporate culture was the sum of all self-evident truths, but Goethe has said it best: "If you cannot sense it, you will never grasp it!"

When a boss starts to think about optimal relations with employees and the best personnel policy, he or she first must look at his/her managers. As a rule at least half the problems are caused by management itself. What do we mean when we talk about "top-quality managers"? What *I* mean is intelligence, talent, education, experience, and everything that falls under that general heading of "personality." That is why I prefer to look into a candidate's eyes rather than at his or her diplomas.

As far as "intelligence" is concerned, what that general term means to me is

☐ The ability to learn and to concentrate;

☐ Quick perception;

☐ A good memory;

☐ Wide-ranging interests.

Narcissistic intellectuals—they who dissect everything, analyze it precisely, and then tell us how bad things are—provide no solutions, practical or otherwise. Usually they do nothing to solve problems, and are the cause of more themselves.

Naturally, schools, companies, and institutes of continuing education all have to work together to provide proper education and training. With regard to universities, an old question recurs: Which is better, more theory or more practical experience? I believe it is more important for universities to convey expectations and attitudes about practical experience. There is a great need for a better understanding of our economic system and for concrete data clearly revealing its advantages over, and superiority to, other systems.

Young people should be encouraged to make real commitments. They need to face reality, and the fact that it must always differ from ideal concepts. Fewer and fewer of them are ready to accept that life, and every meaningful and rewarding activity, always includes a risk. As a society, we need to do a better job of stressing that costs and benefits must be weighed and the law of proportionality applied. These are things that young people today learn far too little about. We need not be surprised, then, that they develop, or fall into, certain ideals and ideologies notably divorced from reality, which carry deception and frustration in their train.

One of the tragedies of life is that experience can be transmitted only to a very limited extent. People have to experience almost everything for themselves. This is why there are, in all honesty, limits to the amount of responsibility that can be conferred on young people—most of them quite simply lack experience. This does not mean that young people cannot be placed in managerial posts quite early on. The "theory of complementarity" applies in this connection: we should put together management teams that contain both older and younger people, with a wide range of knowledge, experience, and temperaments, and let them work with each other.

Nowadays, no one denies that informing managers and employees is an important and necessary part of personnel policy. Employees need to be informed; information provides a sense of security, trust, and identification with the company. Here too, what is important is to find the right "dose" as well as the proper content and form for information. Direct verbal information, conveyed in terms that are easy to understand, is always preferable to complicated texts and leaflets.

In this area, the responsible bosses should be doing more than the personnel and PR departments. Information also must be graded for the various levels of management, while keeping it in mind that top managers need background information. However, for employees, it is often more important to provide direct information about their job and everything that affects them personally rather than to provide detailed informational leaflets on abstract activities or corporate structure.

Employee representatives generally are welcome at Nestlé, and we feel that unions can play a sensible, necessary role in industrial companies. However, it is crucial for unions to play by the rules, the first and foremost of these being "no political arguments at work that impede performance, efficiency, or creativity." Good employee representatives, moreover, not only transmit the desires and problems of the employees. They also can be used to convey information and to solve disagreements, and often they are a source of information on deficiencies in the company or management shortcomings that bosses would never hear about from other sources.

Pay incentives for performance should be favored over a leveling of salaries. It is advantageous to business to have more flexible rules about working times. Fringe benefits should concentrate more on the elderly, the sick, and real emergencies, and less on sprinkling benefits right and left. So-called "entitlements" should not be considered untouchable, and wage policy must be adapted to the mood of the market and the general economic situation rather than to company profits or dividends. As a general rule, in a competitive economy, businesses must make use of every opportunity to increase efficiency, otherwise all their employees will suffer in the long run. However, the necessary measures affecting individual employees should be carried out in a socially responsible manner.

9

Cultivating Corporate Image and Preserving Corporate Culture

Corporate image has become important, both as a basis for a company's long-term activities and also as a means of recruiting capable executives and employees and binding them to the firm.

Here's a thought about corporate image that is too often ignored: the image problems large companies are experiencing nowadays are due more to a lack of trust than to a lack of information.

Moreover, it appears that current methods of disseminating information cannot fully reestablish such trust. For this reason it is imperative that the actual situation of a specific company, its products and its mode of operating, correspond to the information disseminated about the company. In principle, this is very simple. Everyone knows that companies make mistakes from time to time, so if you tell the truth—especially when the truth is unpleasant—you will have something of great value: credibility.

In such cases, public relations tricks or new corporate logos will not help. The first thing to do is to get the company back into shape. No PR department can simply conjure up what a company truly lacks. Concealing company problems no longer works, given the intense coverage of industry by today's media. Instead, a company has to take the offensive and tackle difficulties head-on. Only then can a concept for a corporate image be developed. A corporate image should include everything from the company's products to its management style, way of operating, and personnel policy, as well as brand policy and advertising.

Why should it be so comprehensive? First, because a corporate image is created by such *facts* as size, earnings, position in the market, and above all, a company's products and brands. Second, because there is a connection (too seldom perceived) between corporate image and corporate culture.

For instance, consumers have *some* idea about the nature of Siemens', Coca-Cola's, or IBM's organization, its employees, and their attitudes. The more closely this idea coincides with reality, the better. Whereas the more the corporate image is manipulated so that it no longer corresponds to the facts, the more serious this misconception becomes for a company over the long term. Today, of course, a company's corporate image increasingly is determined by its degree of social responsibility, by whether it actually does things rather than just talks about doing them. Ultimately, corporate image and advertising are closely related, although in a manner that many companies fail to perceive.

If a company's corporate image is based on its products, preferences, and motivations, that image should be reflected in its advertising, for a company's advertising needs to be consistent with its overall corporate image. Otherwise half of the effect is wasted, even if a creative idea should manage to bring higher product sales over the short term.

PR advertising also should be fundamentally in tune with goals related to corporate image. Decisions on sponsoring should be made with a view to their effect on the formation of corporate image over the long term, rather than to flatter egos or to stay in tune with the boss's hobbies.

There is another important aspect of corporate behavior that is too often ignored. Although countless books have been written about how to behave toward customers, I do not know of a single book that advises one on how to deal with suppliers. I have always told Nestlé's advertising, distribution, and purchasing staff "to treat your suppliers the way you want your customers to treat you." A positive attitude of that kind can bring with it real advantages.

Which brings me to the subject of target groups: suppliers, customers and consumers, governments, trade unions, and a company's own employees can have very differing images of the same firm. We all know of companies that, on the whole, have an outstanding corporate image, yet for whom nothing seems to be going right, in one specific area or another.

At the time Nestlé was involved in the infant formula affair, for instance, it came as a deep shock to our Swiss employees. They reacted with righteous anger, which shows that good companies that employ good people are precisely the ones whose employees tend to "circle the wagons" and barricade themselves, while exclaiming, "That's not true! That *can't* be true!" Although this is understandable in human terms, it is all wrong for a company. At Nestlé we took stock dispassionately, started a dialogue with our critics, and gradually eliminated the problem.

DIALOGUE RATHER THAN CIRCULARS

Today, a company's image can be greatly influenced, for better or for worse, by the media. The media have an influence not only on consumers and groups outside the company but also on audiences within the company. When something about me appears in the paper, it is read by far more of our employees than the memos and circulars I address directly to Nestlé's staff. I once referred to this as management "by interview."

A word on the subject of public relations, public affairs, and corporate affairs: for a long time, Nestlé did not understand how to conduct these activities—so very important today—professionally. We learned a great deal at Nestlé from the discussions on the topic of selling infant formula in the third world.

I regard the duties of the people in charge of corporate affairs (including management) as being twofold: on the one hand, these people must provide both the public at large and interest groups (including the critical ones) with information, and they should generate understanding for Nestlé's activities and work. On the other hand—and this is just as important—they should make the firm more sensitive to reactions to corporate decisions by the public or by interest groups.

In and of themselves, the decisions may be correct from an economic or corporate point of view. Yet they sometimes need to be amended, or may require more detailed explanations. This demands intensive involvement on the part of top management, for such duties can be delegated only to a limited extent. In this context I would note that the media, in addition to their job of investigative and critical journalism, have a responsibility to present the facts of the matter and to do so objectively. The valid principle here should be "listen to the other side."

This can create problems, however, for facts are often less important to the media than their own opinions about the facts. In turn, media opinions have a way of virtually *becoming* facts. The media should provide information, criticize where necessary, and contribute to the formation of public opinion. Are these functions always fulfilled today, when the media themselves are battling for market share? Do they not yield too easily to the temptation of sensationalism in order to combat boredom and, in so doing, occasionally distort the facts?

Investigative journalism can contain exaggerations suggestive of a peeping at keyholes. This is a perilous course for the mass media themselves to take, but society must live with it. At any rate, this trend makes it necessary for corporations to adopt an attitude of utter frankness.

Many managers believe it is crucial to develop a strategy for fending off the inquisitiveness of bright journalists and keeping things concealed. Wrong. Sooner or later, such an approach inevitably will lead to renewed distrust, and negative articles about the company will become more rather than less frequent.

There is no doubt that it is more important than ever for corporate managers to have a strong personal commitment to communication. Businesses need executives who can handle this new approach to communication and who have a talent for it. I'm not talking about the latest, ultra-refined techniques, but about the courage and poise to speak frankly about corporate issues, both within the company and to outsiders.

Admittedly, this creates a problem: people in exposed positions are the best channels for messages about the company, because personalizing a message facilitates understanding. However, those people are only one part of a corporation and assume a certain position within the firm for a given time only. Therefore it is imperative to link the corporation to its corporate image and not to personify the company too strongly. The corporate image of a firm must survive, even if the head of the company falls out of an airplane the next day.

I believe the problem can nonetheless be solved if the individual who personifies, or heads, the company is in harmony with its corporate spirit, so that there is no rupture between them. It is only natural for a multinational company with an extensive product range to exhibit a certain blurring of its corporate image. In Germany, for example, there is not only a Nestlé image but also a Maggi image, a Sarotti image, a Nescafé image, and a Herta meat products image, to say nothing of Dallmyr coffee, Alete baby food, or L'Oréal cosmetics.

When it covers many different products, a corporate image can comprise only what the products have in common. Beyond that, the history of the company can perhaps be emphasized, because core values (such as Nestlé quality and tradition) also reflect on the other companies in the Group.

To some extent, the Nestlé logo can be effectively employed for this purpose. Hence, certain basic tenets of the corporate culture of a Swiss company—with our management style and pragmatism—can provide reference values common to all groups of firms. Among them I include realism, speaking frankly, the avoidance of excess, and a certain modesty that lacks neither style nor taste. In our corporate culture, I also include executives who know how to maintain a reasonable balance between their own career objectives and the requisite objectivity about, and dedication to, the company.

There are, of course, trained management professionals, unhampered by values, who wander from company to company, choosing them according to the wages offered or career opportunities. Nestlé, on the other hand, wants managers who keep their power games and intrigues under control (not people who suppress them completely, which would be impossible), and who understand Nestlé's idea of quality that extends from its products and advertising to employee conduct. There would be little call, I believe, for a brochure on Nestlé's corporate culture. Instead, Nestlé employees want to experience it together every day, even though our "little" store has become a very big one. This is how a company can tighten the link between corporate culture and corporate image.

The next step is to differentiate the corporate images of individual companies or products to a certain extent. At Nestlé, we are constantly asking and thinking about to what degree we can reasonably differentiate without harming Nestlé's corporate image. This applies to our brand policy as well. Where should we use the brand name Nestlé? Where does it provide support? In a certain sense you could talk about a hierarchy of values, ranging from the value of images we all have in common (a firm's overall corporate image) to those that can be differentiated (brands, subsidiaries). The replies to the questions just posed will depend on the target groups a company hopes to reach.

Nestlé wants to be an insider, not an outsider, in the countries in which it does business, so as to completely integrate itself into the mentality, habits of consumption, and behavior prevalent there. What effect does that have on Nestlé's corporate image? We try to maintain that image by means of our international brand policy, training at headquarters, and a team of international managers. All of those serve to foster and sustain team spirit, despite specific adaptations to local customs and requirements.

10

The Complex Question of Organizational Authority or Autonomy

An economy's structure and its diverse elements must be able to evolve according to economic criteria while at the same time fostering competitiveness. Some things can be undertaken only by big corporations, others only by regional or small companies. Bearing in mind the prosperity of consumers and citizens, one should not interfere with these structures. A consequence of this is the trend toward concentration, toward bigger business units. Markets are getting bigger; technologies require certain conditions, as do economies of scale—the modern means of streamlining.

However, in highly developed economies there are trends moving in the opposite direction. In spite of pessimistic forecasts, there is still great diversity in the economy. There are now more services offered, which automatically changes the structure of the economy. There are suppliers, specialists, and niches. Today there is no one, generic "consumer," nor are there six or seven different lifestyles but rather almost atomized, individualized consumers. This provides opportunities for many different offers. There are even opportunities implicit in today's technology: with the help of computers, even small businesses can compete using modern means and methods. They can become mechanized and can communicate. Finally, the fact that more borders now are open is also important. This permits even smaller firms to jump borders. Before, a big company needed a whole staff and a great deal of know-how if it was to overcome the many obstacles to foreign trade. Now, as more and more countries open up their markets, a greater number of varied companies will be doing business internationally.

What else can be done to reinforce this trend toward variety, toward a mixture of companies and diversity? Fewer laws and deregulation would help to keep reasonable structures in place. No one can claim that small and medium-sized businesses are dying out because big corporations are stealing their thunder. Rather they close down because they cannot figure out modern legislation or afford staffs of people to enable them to fulfill all of the legal requirements that legislators and government heap on them nowadays.

Less government intervention in the economy is another very essential point—especially, looking around the world, in view of how many things need government approval and how many government contacts a company must have just in order to do business. In many countries, having an office for such contacts is not an option but a matter of sheer survival.

This seems the right place to consider how much provision for welfare we really need as a society, so as not to neglect social protection for the needy. Or consider environmental problems: if society solves environmental problems only through laws and ordinances, the result will be a jumble of laws yet again, or interventions and regulations that will tend to make it harder for every small and medium-sized company and self-employed person to keep up with things. We should therefore try to let the market settle as many problems as possible, by means of incentives and prices, and leave the rest, that really needs it, to regulations and laws.

BUYING SERVICES OUTSIDE

What can big corporations do to foster autonomy within the firm, or to encourage small, independent companies outside the firm? Big companies can make a whole series of contributions by purchasing outside of the company goods or services that really are not part of the task of a big corporation.

We have all sinned in this regard, and many businesses are still sinning. All the services that do not belong in a big company—be it market research or advertising, the fleet of vehicles or the company restaurant, trade jobs or repairs, financial services, the company bank, architects, laundry—can be placed outside and purchased in the market.

That is what should be done from the point of view of a market economy, for then there is competition for those things. It is also the right thing to do, because it creates a variety of opportunities for self-employed businesspeople. It also has the advantage of freeing top managers in big companies from wasting their time with questions that really have nothing to do with their own business. I call this "varying fixed costs," which also makes sense from a managerial point of view, for then the company is not burdened with fixed cost structures. Therefore I see in this area good opportunities for big corporations to foster innovation and autonomy outside the company.

At Nestlé too, one of the reasons for our success certainly is the fact that our operations are decentralized. We have given even more staff jobs to the line; we have integrated our business units more closely with other functions, so that they can act independently. And we have centers of excellence that absolutely do not need to be located in Vevey on Lake Geneva, but can be anywhere in the world where people understand more about them. Like most companies, Nestlé now has fewer hierarchical levels, broader sectors of responsibility, and so forth. Many of our employees—not just managers—can be mobilized through the use of various concepts. Two of these are "management by commitment" and "employee involvement." Nestlé wants to foster a new type of management with that formula, as well as a more innovative, better climate at work.

At Nestlé, when we are in doubt as to what should be done at the top and what should be done lower down the line, our principle is: do it at a lower level. A person would have to offer some pretty impressive arguments to convince me that something can be done better or cheaper by any of the people at the top.

There is also another point of view: in York, England, at Nestlé's recently acquired Rowntree, our employees have started something they call "team working." In specific areas—not everywhere—employees organize their work themselves, not in the sense of an assembly line, as they do in the automotive industry, but rather in an essentially more pragmatic manner. When I asked how it worked, I was told that costs had stayed about the same (which says that expecting the firm to save money this way is illusory), but that the workers were more satisfied and motivated because they had greater decision-making power. Moreover there were considerably fewer damaged goods, and quality had improved.

I do not want to wax sentimental, and I feel I must warn against the idyllic picture some descriptions paint. Self-management is possible only in a few, small areas. But there are gradual steps a company can take in that direction that are in its best interest and will also bring employees more satisfaction, so that they can work more autonomously and happily.

Here I am talking about the lowest executive levels; companies never take good enough care of this stratum of management. At the top, people grasp such things intellectually. The people recruited for the lowest executive levels, however, are the least prepared for their managerial jobs. Yet these are the executives who, in the plant, on-site, are considered "Mr. Nestlé." They represent the company to outsiders.

BUILDING TRUST

One thing is clear: In order to achieve greater autonomy, companies need fewer rules and a smaller administration. I still remember my arrival in Vevey, at a time when Nestlé still had departments that laid down the proper length for a ruler. Of course one can always justify such things, but executives should realize that their firms simply can no longer do such things, and sweep all such "justifications" off their desks. I prefer to select my managers more carefully.

Mistakes are often made when trying to balance control and trust. I believe that you can trust people more than managers traditionally have. I would rather be cheated in two cases out of a hundred than forgo the real advantages produced by trusting people more. Outside the company, new opportunities for autonomous jobs exist for those working on computers at home. There are many additional opportunities to mobilize people by using self-employed sales representatives or by entrusting work downstream to independent companies.

With regard to the possibility of labor (i.e., the trade unions) developing a culture of job autonomy, I will venture no predictions, for I do not know enough about the unions. In general, though, trade unions should certainly also change their policies. Collective agreements should be less rigid; the unions should be more flexible and should have more links to the company, and they should adapt better to various situations.

Trade unions could only undertake all such changes hesitantly. I can understand that, for a trade union has to have a global approach:

It needs general guidelines, and loses some of its control and perspective if adaptation to individual companies is carried too far. Moreover, the fact that shorter working hours seem to have created an enormous potential for self-employment and for more independence, with more time available to work in the "shadow" economy, is perhaps not what its proponents had originally intended. However, with shorter working hours, there will be many more opportunities of different kinds.

I would not dare to give a confident reply to the question of how much influence co-determination, laws on shop organization, and such things can have on job autonomy. Surely, however, the feeling of being able to contribute and also of having something to say, even through a committee, provides a good deal of impetus.

There are, of course, certain limits to what big corporations can do. Many people come to work for us because they want a relatively ordered, secure professional life, in which they can apply what they have learned in a sensible, professional manner. Often, such people want to optimize their private lives after working hours, during vacations, and on weekends, more than they want independence. That amounts to seclusion, not autonomy, hedonism rather than responsibility. There will always be differences among people; they will always like different things and dislike different things. And yet, somehow, things always seem to work out midway between the herd instinct and the thirst for freedom.

Upbringing, training, a change in mentalities and modified consciousness will be required to promote a culture of job autonomy. We will all (parents, schools, and businesses) have to work together, sponsoring seminars and continuing education programs, so that offers of autonomous jobs inside and outside companies will be accepted more readily and more people will want to work at them, with all the advantages that will procure for society and for the economy as well.

Yet job autonomy should not be confused with an excessive pluralism, or a dismantling of authority. The relationship between leadership and autonomy is a subject that needs to be examined more closely. Certainly, leadership, or management, has become more difficult today, first, because authority is (thank God) no longer automatically acknowledged, and second because there is less true consensus in society these days; pluralism has, in part, degenerated into polarization. Therefore the challenge before us is to find new forms of leadership that will be readily accepted rather than forced through. Opportunities for finding a new balance, while preserving leadership, do exist; they will result from interactions among autonomy, delegation, decentralization, a participatory management style, and undisputed authority. A certain fighting spirit will be called for if the best solution is to emerge victorious from the struggle.

Of course, the most important social function of a company is to offer on the market goods, products, and services that can stand up to competition. Everything else must be secondary. So while I am all for business ethics and social responsibility, I am opposed to all mere ethical and social blathering.

11

Ethics and the Economy

Since the free-market economic system is "ethical" in the broad sense that it does good things for mankind, one might say that businesspeople who do their best within the system are, from an objective point of view, acting morally and ethically. Everything harmful to our economic system would then be wrong and immoral, because it would reduce the beneficial effect of the economic system on society.

A businessperson's most important moral and ethical responsibility is to support our economic system, since he or she is convinced it is the best. Today businesspeople can no longer retreat into their private realms and follow Goethe's famous dictum: "Blessed is he who, without hate, withdraws from the world."

It is a mistake to advocate social or welfare policies before your company has earned a profit or, worse, regardless of company profits. In this regard I could cite many sad examples, provided by state-owned companies in countries with total job security, positive employee benefits, and wage policies. Consider the losses that must, ultimately, be financed by taxpayers. Indeed, not only must the losses be absorbed, but the taxes that profitable firms would ordinarily be paying are missing as well.

I can find no trace of ethics, morality, or civic responsibility in such examples. But of course, the social balance sheets of such companies look very good. A saying that I like to quote is certainly apposite here: "The opposite of good is good intentions."

A reporter once asked me whether I had any morals. I replied: "When we are talking about things like economic principles, you should leave my morals aside. You should rely on the fact that the system we're living in gives the best results. For you will find the whole spectrum of humanity among businessmen, from the good to the bad. If the system depended on everyone being moral, then we could abandon the system. The system itself must contain moral, ethical values. And what's more, I actually do have a set of personal morals."

THE MORALITY OF THE MARKET

It is a fact that every economic system, no matter how good, contains weaknesses; and there will always be abuses, for it is human beings who are at work. Therefore one must strive to achieve a balanced outlook and not proceed on the basis of a priori principles, like all of those who condemn the whole system after pointing out a few of its weaknesses. Nonetheless, an economic system can certainly be improved by appropriate moral and ethical behavior on the part of the businesspeople acting within it.

Candidates for upper-level management positions should always be required to show not only specialized skills and executive ability but also a corresponding sense of moral and ethical responsibility. The same is true for candidates in politics, industry, and other institutions as well. If this combination is lacking in the top people, the effect on society is likely to be negative—indeed, in some cases, dangerous. Familiar extreme examples drawn from political life are people like Hitler and Stalin, but in business life too, misdeeds do occur: bank failures, misuse of insider information, bribery, and scandals of all kinds.

For this reason, people and departments that elect or appoint others to positions of responsibility—be they citizens, shareholders, or members of the legislature, of boards of directors, or of advisory boards—have an obligation, when selecting people to promote or back, to scrutinize with great care their ability and willingness to take moral responsibility. The media and the public also must exercise a critical, supervisory function.

Although we all approve of it, I would make a brief comment about this so-called supervisory function. The "purist" attitudes encountered today should give us pause. They are in fact tainted with hypocrisy or with a simple desire to increase some medium's circulation. For instance, mere media snooping, during the election of the president of the United States, has become commonplace. What was once termed "keyhole" reporting, or snooping, is now given the far nobler title of "investigative journalism." To such "investigative" reporters I would like to say: "Let him [or her] who is without sin among you be the first to cast a stone at her [or him]."

As I said, I willingly accept the critical scrutiny of the media, even with all its limitations, because the public and the press can do much to promote moral thinking within a company. But let us never forget that the profit motive is the controlling element in a market economy. Ethics must not simply write it off as egotism or greed, for profit is the driving force behind our economic system. This is precisely the fact that disturbs so many people and leads them to the attack again and again. I remember a discussion I had with a sociology professor many years ago. We had disagreed, and I had brought out all my arguments. At the end he said, "Mr. Maucher, I've understood now; nevertheless, inside I'm still against it." That is the really tragic thing about intellectuals: they simply cannot, or will not, understand the profit mechanism.

In my opinion, one must search for a reasonable line of demarcation: where does healthy egoism end and unethical behavior begin? This is a perilous question. In this area there are no absolute and eternally valid criteria, not even in a free-market economy with a social component or a market economy with a marked environmental orientation. A market economy is not a rigid thing. Its boundaries, opportunities and emphases must be redefined constantly, as we see happening today with the efforts to reconcile the economy and the environment. But the question that always arises is how far such ethical requirements can go without destroying the entire system.

Of course if the assumption of ethical and moral responsibility does not cost a firm anything from a cost/benefit point of view, then companies should act accordingly. This applies to interpersonal relations, for example, where much can be improved without any expense.

If on the other hand additional costs are incurred over the short term, but advantages accrue to the firm over the long term, such action is in the company's interest as well. Here ethical behavior is consistent with long-term business interests, especially when current earnings permit such a course of action. Many examples can be drawn upon from the personnel sector. Most employees realize that we are all in the same boat in the long run—which does not prevent any of us from constantly arguing about short-term problems.

If a certain ethical or moral action would result in short- or long-term costs for the firm with no additional advantages, it then becomes considerably more difficult for a company to make a decision. A typical example would be voluntary environmental protection measures. As a citizen, I might be in favor of measures that go far beyond those applied in our factories today. As a citizen, I might support laws that would lead to more effective environmental protection at the expense of other things. (After all, you can't do everything at once.) I might, as a member of a professional association, be in favor of a specific mode of behavior for that industry: for instance, that different sewage treatment facilities be installed, that fewer pollutants be emitted into the atmosphere, and so on. If these things are achieved throughout an industry, an association, or an international organization, then they will have no effect on competition. The individual company will suffer no disadvantages, and the measures in question can be supported by businesspeople with a clear conscience.

But if an individual company decides to adopt a certain mode of behavior, knowing that its competitors will not go along with it, that is an entirely different matter. Nevertheless, I feel that it is proper for big corporations with healthy earnings to be the first to implement useful measures, given a firm's general responsibility to society.

When a measure involves excessive costs, the company that decides to implement it may no longer be competitive and may, consequently, be doomed to failure—with all that entails for its employees and shareholders. In such a case, behavior that is moral and ethical on the surface will prove to be immoral in the final analysis, or at least to result in a reduction in earnings. This however is a matter for the owner to decide, not a hired manager. An owner may agree to a reduction in earnings, which would be like paying additional taxes, or he may refuse to do so—which should not be held against him.

Here the hired manager has a special responsibility, since it is always easy to spend someone else's money. The hired manager's motivations often differ from those of the owner. Frequently, hired managers are considered good managers on the basis of expenditures only marginally related to business activities. In the final analysis, however, such managers are merely nursing their own vanities and hobbies.

I am referring here to the whole problem of donations, corporate sponsorship, and support for cultural events. What are the general obligations of big corporations? How do such expenditures serve their long-term interests, goodwill, and reputations? When does the matter become a problem with regard to corporate goals and the legitimate interests of shareholders? These are difficult questions that we managers must confront every day.

If executives are convinced that, in most cases, moral and ethical behavior by corporate management is in the long-term interest of any company and makes secure a firm's income, corporate image, and viability, then it makes sense for them to support such behavior through voluntary codes, appropriate consciousness-raising, and public monitoring of conduct. There are important roles to be played by the media and by scholars working at universities and elsewhere in strengthening awareness of, and sensitivity to, corporate responsibility. When such awareness finally becomes a part of our common heritage, neutrality with regard to competition will be restored. That in turn will enable businesses to make better overall contributions to the community.

It has become fashionable to forget a firm's moral duties and obligations toward its shareholders. Those duties include safeguarding shareholders' property, ensuring profitability while taking risk factors into account, and providing accurate information that enables shareholders (or owners who do not act in a managerial capacity) to make informed decisions or to facilitate the planning of their own investments and capital expenditures.

Here, too, problems arise. For example, the interests of shareholders differ: there are those who invest for the long term, and those who are interested in quick profits. Some want higher dividends, some larger allocations to reserves, depending on their tax situations or current cash requirements. Shareholders' concern for the share price also plays a role, as do the conditions for equity increases or the fact that Nestlé's registered shares are held in majority by Swiss, which implies that shares are harder to sell and their market value lower. Even these few cases demonstrate how difficult it is to set and hold a course of moral and ethical behavior with regard to shareholders, one that will simultaneously serve everyone's interests.

Socially responsible behavior toward the staff, as well as support and training, are in the long-term interest of everyone involved. As a rule, conflicts arise only with regard to short-term claims or in connection with efficiency measures, dismissals, or plant shutdowns. Such measures are necessary from an overall economic standpoint, since without them the prosperity and increased productivity of the past one or two centuries could not have been achieved. However, the measures must be accompanied by generous social benefits, severance packages, job transfers, retraining, timely information, and the establishment of reasonable deadlines. Few will disagree that companies have an obligation to do those things.

In the case of some other issues, however, it is sometimes difficult to know the right thing to do:

- Should young employees be given opportunities for advancement, or should older employees be protected?
- Should there be large differences in pay between individual groups, with corresponding performance incentives, or should a firm's goal be a leveling of wages in the interest of solidarity, fairness, and performance?
- Should retirement and health benefits be given priority, or should salaries continually be increased, with less job security for employees?
- Is "benevolent patriarchal" management right or wrong?
- Is a strict corporate culture, the kind that prescribes a certain line of conduct and that many praise so highly today, a good thing, or is it better to accept a completely pluralistic, liberalized mode of behavior?

When it comes to questions about product quality, protecting consumers, and advertising methods, should a company produce any and every product that consumers want? (Consider cigarettes, alcohol, and the debates over socially acceptable consumption.) Some groups claim to know the answer, but consumers often do not agree. Remember the controversy about the reasonable use and proper marketing of infant formula, whose use is simply a necessity in many cases? There are no simple solutions, especially in the third world. This is an issue that could be discussed and analyzed endlessly, in terms of moral and ethical responsibility.

A major customer once said to me, "Well, what am I supposed to do? I can't exploit consumers, because of the competition; and I can't exploit my staff, because of the union. So I have no alternative but to exploit my suppliers." Short-term aggressive behavior toward suppliers is not advantageous to any company in the long run. What pays off in the end is cooperative, civilized conduct, geared to long-term relationships especially with a company's partners, advertising agencies, banks, and suppliers of merchandise and commodities.

This is precisely the advantage of long-term relationships. Sometimes, subordinates who are looking for immediate, visible successes do not see that or do not show proper consideration for such things. Corporate management has the task of maintaining a certain equilibrium in this sector.

Another subject that needs to be mentioned in this context as well is moral, ethical behavior during acquisitions: questionable takeover practices or methods of financing hostile takeovers.

Supplying honest information inside and outside the company also is important. Of course, in a free market, the amount and extent of information a company supplies needs to be restricted enough so that competitors will not be able to make complete sense of it, or the firm could end up with a strategic disadvantage. Where information is concerned, managers are always caught on the horns of a dilemma: one "horn" being the needs of the public, the other their own need for secrecy. Under this heading I also want to mention bribery and nepotism: to what extent should a multinational adapt to local customs or, alternatively, insist on applying its own general principles?

What, in fact, is ethical and moral conduct? Is it sufficient for companies' behavior to accord with people's general consensus as to "decent" behavior? Can a working ethic be arrived at in a purely utilitarian manner, or is there also an absolute, dogmatic, theological ethic? Although I do not believe myself capable of answering such questions conclusively, I would like to offer two thoughts as the basis for further reflection:

1. "All creatures," said the Stoic philosopher Epictetus, "are created in such a way that they do everything for their own sakes. Zeus made the nature of the rational animal such that no one can obtain any personal benefit without simultaneously making some contribution to the general welfare. As a result, the welfare of mankind is not undermined simply because someone acts in his own best interest."

2. Some modern behaviorists and ethologists trace all ethical and moral modes of behavior back to the survival techniques of certain species, including human beings. For example, the famous behaviorist Irenäus Eibl-Eibelsfeld stated that the altruistic inclinations of the human race and its benevolent behavior were to be attributed solely to mankind's instinct to care for its offspring, which is necessary for the survival of the species.

I will now offer a final few words about the supposed incompatibility between business efficiency on the one hand and, on the other, humanitarian actions and that tolerance we value so highly today. I am confident that, the more mankind takes the long view, the more opportunities there will be to reduce to a common denominator such seemingly opposed things as humanitarian action and business efficiency.

At Nestlé's headquarters in Vevey, we hold seminars that are attended by people from all over the world, from Japan to Argentina. I am always pleased to observe that these seminars result in greater comprehension of, and tolerance for, different cultures. This is one way, and a good one, for multinationals to build tolerance and understanding among the very different peoples of the world.

The question of whether this spirit can be captured by writing down corporate principles or ideals crops up repeatedly. At Nestlé we have never done so, for two reasons.

First, such concepts are so similar as to be all but interchangeable, and thus lose any relevance for individual firms. Goethe wrote "Let man be noble, helpful, and good" long before anyone tried to put corporate ideals down in writing. Second, if the formulation of corporate principles is overly specific, those principles will no longer prove applicable to the great variety of a multinational's products, subsidiaries, and cultures. In any case, I think what is most important is to *live* a corporate culture, to set examples with it, and then from time to time to talk about it. This is the way to develop a real corporate culture and basic principles, so that employees will understand which sort of conduct is highly prized and which will not be tolerated.

There was a good reason for me to choose credibility as one of my most important management principles. A manager must expect to be questioned closely the following day as to what he said the day before and to acquit himself admirably. The extent to which such things need to be controlled from outside the company is another matter. I believe the controlling should be left to the market, consumers, and laws. The exercise of moral control from any quarter beyond those three interests me very little.

As a final thought on this important subject of ethics in business, I share with you a Japanese saying: "Love your enemies, but run a bit faster than they do!"

12

Morality
or Profits?

The topic of ethics in business is increasingly becoming the center of a broad debate, a debate not at all welcome in many circles. Some feel that there is an insurmountable antimony, an irreconcilable contradiction between the two concepts of morality and profits. It is odd that this doubt has appeared at exactly the same time as the failure of the socialist ideologies and economies has become clear. Are people trying to use ethical and moral misgivings to overturn our economic system, now that the superiority of the capitalist system and the collapse of command economies are matters of fact? Or, after many years of growing prosperity (within a framework of a general inflation of entitlements), is the question that now arises simply one about the ethical dimension of economic activity?

Here are a few theses that will perhaps serve as an outline of my point of view:

- For citizens and consumers, a market economy produces the best results when it is combined with anti-monopolistic regulations and a sociopolitical component, especially if such values as freedom and prosperity are ranked high by the public. The free-market system also creates better social conditions and the requisite funds for constructing a social safety net for the weak and the disadvantaged.

- In terms of the best distribution, control, and decentralization of power, a market economy is the best economic complement to democracy and to the principle of subsidiarity.

- No one has found a more efficient mechanism of civic control than profit, the oft-disparaged and -despised guiding principle of a market economy.

- In a competitive economy, a corporation derives its legitimacy from the simple fact that it offers consumers products attractive

121

to them in terms of quality, service, variety, and price. This generates a profit, ensuring the company's existence over the long term and permitting it to develop as required and to produce a return for investors.

☐ Every other economic system has turned out to be less satisfactory than the free market, as long as the comparison is made between realities, not reality on the one hand and Utopia on the other.

☐ The previous item is so obviously true that attempts now are being made to incorporate elements of a free market into the socialist systems formerly under central control. There have even been attempts to impose the entire free-market system in toto.

Having closely observed the effect our free-enterprise system has on mankind, I have concluded that it is ethical, and that a businessperson who conforms to the system, is, from an objective point of view, acting in an ethical and moral manner. That is why I reject the supposed antithesis between morality and profits. It is also why I ask myself, from time to time, whether the search for the so-called ethical dimension of business is anything more than a desire to confirm old prejudices and doubts that have a merely emotional foundation.

No System Is Perfect

Do we now enjoy the best of everything in the best of all possible worlds? Of course we don't. Human beings will always make mistakes, and no system is so perfect as to offer no opportunity for abuse. A market economy may candidly claim to be independent of the altruistic moral behavior (however defined) of any of its participants. It is so successful precisely because it is devoid of any such unrealistic prerequisite.

As the controlling element of a market economy, profit cannot be wished away, and every attempt to limit it by means of standards, legislation, and codes, makes the market that much less efficient. However, a free-market economy is an open system that reacts to criticism and is capable of being corrected. How far outside intervention can go without destroying the system's ability to function is a question of measure. For instance, as a citizen (and also in my own long-term interests as a businessperson), I have been an advocate of clear and sensibly handled antitrust legislation.

Similarly, none of us can find arguments against legal measures protecting society's weaker elements, the environment, consumers, and so on, as long as they do not radically disrupt the market mechanism or unfairly aid one competitor among many by granting it artificial privileges. Yet even here, politicians and citizens are called upon to remain within bounds and not immediately combat every unimportant and temporary inequality with the heavy artillery of regulations. I have witnessed very many improvements within individual branches of industry, and even in the entire economy, that came into being through competition and without the acute pressure of legislation. But this happens only when a certain capacity for judgment exists in all parties.

There are no absolute and eternally valid criteria in this area either, and it is the system's very ability to change that constantly forces us to reflect anew on demands and problems. I realize that this attitude of mine goes against current trends. When I see that masochistic bewilderment that finds its outlet in whining Letters to the Editor, even in reputable newspapers, I sometimes find myself wondering where people's common sense and perspective have gone. They are victims of the "subito" syndrome, the attitude that demands that every problem be solved *immediately,* as soon as it is identified by this or that group, regardless of the consequences. Much of this, surely, can be explained by the impatience of youth; however, people in responsible positions would do well to maintain a long-term outlook, come what may.

ACCEPTANCE IS NECESSARY

Finally, it seems to me that ethical and moral behavior by corporate managers also is mandatory, because it safeguards acceptance of our economic system across a wide spectrum of the public. In a democracy, there is a continuing pressure to justify every arrangement made. While capitalism, thanks to its ability to create wealth, brings in its wake many social benefits, ethically correct behavior contributes to dampening moral criticism of the market economy and to preventing the formation of a majority hostile to the system. I am terming such criticism "moral," although it is characterized by grotesquely exaggerated demands made on an economic arrangement conceived and carried out by human beings, with all their foibles and failings, and by a condemnation of the entire free-market system simply because each part cannot meet all of society's requirements all the time.

To paraphrase Churchill, I maintain that "a free-market economy is the worst of all systems, with the exception of all the others." In other words, before making a hasty judgment one should take a moment to consider all of the possible alternatives. All of those critics who, because of the splinter in the eye of the free-enterprise system, ignore the beam in the eye of every planned economy, should reflect on the following: the last report on development published by the World Bank ranked 120 countries according to their pro capita income. Switzerland headed the list; Ethiopia came last.

Well over half the countries above the average were democracies. Capitalism as an economic form seems to lead, sooner or later, to democracy, just as the planned economy inevitably ends in a totalitarian system. It is the lack of democratic controls, the centralization of decision-making power (with the resulting deleterious effect on the individual's sense of responsibility and willingness to work), that lead to misuse of political power and to economic decline in totalitarian systems.

The developments in Eastern Europe and the political and economic collapse of the Soviet Union demonstrate that, in the final analysis, economic forces can break up and renovate "incrusted" political structures. Criticism of the market should take that into account as well. To my mind, every businessperson should make it his or her job, as a citizen, to stand up for democratic capitalism.

HAVING A SOCIALLY RESPONSIBLE ATTITUDE TOWARD EMPLOYEES

Without immediately and conclusively assessing individual principles, I would like to examine the ethical content of some principles we apply at Nestlé. Customers and products are more important to us than systems, and that is certainly in the long-term interests of Nestlé's business. However, it also affects a whole range of people especially interested in our company: shareholders, employees, consumers, society in general. The focus of attention for our shareholders is certainly the long-term security of the capital they invested, as well as the earning of appropriate interest—in other words, a successful company.

It would be hard for me to imagine that a company could succeed in our branch of industry if it failed to manufacture products for strongly divergent, socially and ethically varied needs; nor could it survive without employing the right people in the right places. Shareholders also have a right to demand straightforward information that will enable them to make the decisions they are entitled to make (as to whether to buy or sell shares) knowledgeably. If Nestlé wants to fulfill its responsibility to look after the interests of its more than 100,000 shareholders, it must not forget that those interests often diverge.

The demands that our employees make, all 200,000 or so of them around the world, are clear. And it goes without saying that a socially responsible attitude toward company personnel, especially when it comes to its demands and opportunities for continuing education, is in the interest of both parties.

RESPONSIBILITY TO CONSUMERS

Consumers of Nestlé products and, more often, their self-appointed "protectors," sometimes make contradictory demands, and those demands raise troubling questions.

☐ Should a company meet requests for obviously unhealthy but socially tolerated products (alcohol, cigarettes), especially when there is a clear demand for them?

☐ How far should advertising go in its search for impressive pictures and slogans?

☐ Who determines what is defensible with regard to product safety and whether it is necessary to describe the most nonsen-

sical misuses of a product as part of the instructions and warn-
ings about its use? (I'm thinking here of anecdotes like the one
about the lady who tried to dry her cat in a microwave oven and
sued the manufacturer when the cat died—and won.)

☐ Where does one make the proper ethical tradeoff between quality and the investment that must necessarily be made in it?

☐ How do I behave when an interest group or political party tries
to lay down the law for socially correct consumption in a third
world country?

I know from many of my own experiences, from contacts both
with doctors and with sales figures, that the consumers concerned do
not share the opinion of their self-styled "advocates" by any means.
However, I also know that abuses really are occurring, with tragic results for the people concerned.

BEHAVIOR TOWARD THE PUBLIC

In this area too, many troubling questions present themselves:

☐ As the head of a big corporation, how am I to proceed when I
receive urgent appeals from very well-meaning organizations
and individuals to use the company's entire know-how, production capacity, and technology in a campaign to stop hunger?

☐ Society wants corporations to pay taxes. Am I entitled to keep
them as low as possible by giving the corporation a sensible legal structure and thus improving the corporation's financial situation in the interests of our shareholders and employees as well
as consumers?

☐ How far should Nestlé go when it is asked to join humanitarian,
cultural, or academic committees? Should we just provide financing, or should we allow employees to help during working
hours?

□ To what extent can a company put to use its particular know-how on political committees, without running the risk of being attacked as a lobbyist for its own cause?

□ How should a company conduct itself when third parties arouse nationalist passions so as to combat a planned takeover that is in the interest of both the companies concerned?

□ How much information can Nestlé be expected to provide to the public? After all, a company can't be expected to place itself at a notable competitive disadvantage.

□ Do I have the right to impose principles that seem proper to Nestlé on other cultural circles, where people may feel that our principles run counter to their own traditions (for instance, the promoting of members of one's own family)? Where does the border run between a desirable adaptation to local mentality on the one side and, on the other, a complete abandonment of the corporation's sense of its own identity?

VEGETARIAN TIGERS?

We have already seen that interests coincide far more often in the long run than might at first appear likely from a worm's-eye point of view. For example, long-term corporate policy makes it easier for company employees to act toward business partners, advertising agencies, banks, and suppliers in a way that shows ethical thinking yet corresponds to company interests. The lack of pressure to show illusory, short-term gains prevents massive plays for market power, and also keeps business partners from being put under brutal pressure.

The fact that Nestlé has always championed commodity agreements is explained by similar considerations. First, such agreements make it possible for us to purchase coffee and cacao beans of the desired quality, at prices that fluctuate within a certain range, thus making it easier to calculate production costs and prices. Second, they also help producing countries to obtain the foreign exchange they need to develop, thereby helping to make the livelihood of local farmers more secure, to prevent rural exodus, and to lower the financial contributions the industrialized world has to make as aid to development. This adds up to so many visible advantages that Nestlé can with a clear conscience ask the customer to pay a somewhat higher price. Unfortunately, it seems that, at the moment, there exist contradictory short-term interests on both sides, thus blocking progress in commodity negotiations.

There are neither more nor fewer violations of ethical and moral principles in business than in any other field of human endeavor. Therefore I do not think that the economy needs to subject itself to a particularly probing examination of conscience. Nor does it seem advisable to me to hamper the fundamental driving forces that keep the system going, even if it is done out of respect for moral principles that are anything but absolute or eternally valid.

For when we compare the total advantages for the whole of society (and they are indisputably positive), we must ask ourselves whether it really is the cleverest solution to knock the wild beast on the head and turn the tiger into a vegetarian. I believe we businesspeople are justified in questioning the motives of the critics of our economic system and asking, "Why does egotism have such a bad reputation?" Does the criticism spring from the Christian ideal of tolerance or the dictates of altruism, or is it perhaps a sign of a driving force almost as strong—namely, envy—that frequently disguises itself as egalitarianism?

The market economy has absolutely no reason to refuse to discuss its ethics or to maintain that they are irrelevant. There is no doubt that democratic capitalism, like any other system conceived by man, could be improved. As the example of the Nestlé Group's corporate policies shows, these can be drawn up so as to foster conduct that meets ethical requirements while, at the same time, being in the long-term interest of the company.

I very much doubt whether the best solution to each situation is always the one we choose, or even whether we always weigh both sides of a question with the necessary thoroughness and expert knowledge. I am convinced, however, that a corporate policy like Nestlé's gives those in responsible positions the necessary leeway to include in their considerations the ethical dimensions of their actions. If a manager has been carefully chosen, trained, and promoted, he or she will be well prepared to start walking the high-wire between divergent and often unclear interests.

THE NECESSARY SOCIAL COMPONENT OF A MARKET ECONOMY

Does a market economy need to have a social component? Or, to put it differently, is the market, per se, defensible as the guiding principle of economic activity? Is the way the market affects the whole economy, and all those involved in it, efficient? My reader, I'm sure, will not blame a necessarily pragmatic businessperson for approaching a few theories on the subject from that standpoint.

If by "the regulation of economic activity" we mean something more positive than a socially just policy that ends up redistributing not so much wealth as poverty, then none can deny that a market economy and capitalism are clearly superior to other systems. How else but through those mechanisms can human beings act out their latent desire to improve the material conditions of their lives? How else can the thousands and thousands of conflicts of interest that occur daily be resolved, if not by decentralized decisions based on individual preferences?

Japan's development after the Meiji restoration of 1868 seems revealing to me. Although for the most part there was nothing in Japanese thought or civilization to profoundly incline them toward Adam Smith's body of ideas, responsible Japanese seem simply to have adopted the idea of a market economy then prevailing in Great Britain (and still prevailing there today, I trust!). The economic, political, and cultural results certainly look good when compared with other systems and utopias.

Even if economic activity is restricted to the limited function of "prosperity for everyone" and if such elements of differentiation as promotion of performance through competition, motivation, or self-actualization are eliminated, a market economy comes off incomparably better than all collective or self-governing models. To my mind, a market economy's ability to create and increase wealth is its own justification.

Yet as a citizen, another element also seems important to me: I would not like to live in a country that limited my freedom or that of my fellow citizens. A part of that freedom—and not the least important part—springs from a self-determined exchange of goods and services. When this element of economic self-determination is missing from a society, there is neither freedom nor wealth.

Admittedly, we all know of countries whose systems seriously encroach on the political liberties of their citizens without hampering their economic activities. Yet no one who has seen the results of government tutelage in politics and economics will be surprised to see, within a very short time, the will to work, the wealth of inventiveness, and a personal sense of responsibility replaced by corruption, the reign of shirkers, and unrestrained exploitation of every position of power. A government unlimited by institutional boundaries has a natural tendency to intervene further and further into every area of society. Yet wherever it grants economic leeway, whether out of insight or necessity, the market economy brings a dynamic to bear that shrinks the government's sphere of influence.

SOCIALIST UTOPIA

"All democracies are capitalist; no democracy is socialist. There are many capitalist societies that are not democratic." So says Peter L. Berger in his book *The Capitalist Revolution* (Basic Books, New York, 1986), which is well worth reading. How could it be otherwise? Modern socialist governments control all the means of retaining power, their administration being unrestricted by parliamentary controls or limitations. *State-controlled economies,* to me a far more accurate term than *planned economy,* inevitably limit freedom in the end. The last few years have taught us all that populations refuse to put up with that forever.

There is a saying in Eastern Europe: "They [the authorities] pretend to pay us, so we pretend to work." The unsatisfactory output of countries with state-controlled economies is only too apparent. The governments clearly had a great deal of trouble just trying to satisfy their citizens' basic needs. As was obvious after the collapse of the socialist states, their health services, construction methods, and even food supplies in no way met the standards for these in the industrialized Western countries. Most of the products that Western consumers find with ease in every supermarket fall into the category of "luxury goods" in Eastern Europe—if the items are available at all. With the exception of the arms those countries produced and their raw materials, scarcely a single product would satisfy Western requirements.

To me, it is also interesting that a new class has evolved on the road to Eastern Europe's supposed classless society: the socialist bureaucracy. The communist elite claimed privileges for themselves that people in the West would have a hard time even imagining, and which seem to confirm the truth behind Leon Trotsky's resigned remark: "Whenever someone has something to share, he won't forget himself." Although this nightmare now seems to be ending, changing a colossus like the former Soviet Union into a number of market economies overnight is sure to be a task on a par with those faced by Hercules.

I do not deny that the socialist Utopia as envisioned by Marx and Lenin (not the real thing) contained an indisputably attractive element. I am thinking of egalitarianism, the doing away with overly large differences in incomes and lifestyles. Yet the fact is that such differences are inherent in the capitalist system, given the effect of the market. Hampering, or even worse, stopping them, would cause the loss of a valuable signal and make the free-enterprise system as a whole less efficient.

The news that the Marxist notion of an "impoverishment of the masses" has finally been discredited should by now have reached even the departments of sociology at our universities. Yet what about the differences in income that, interestingly enough, have quickly become, in some political discussions, intrinsic "inequalities" or even "injustices"? Are they more marked in a free-enterprise system, perhaps even solidifying along class lines?

The "horrible human consequences" of capitalism are often illustrated by using the example of the Industrial Revolution in Great Britain. People indisputably have trouble coming to terms with such fundamental changes. Let us not forget, however, that the Industrial Revolution took place over a limited period of time and produced widespread improvements in living conditions. Fortunately, it is now possible for us to gain a clearer picture of this gigantic upheaval through the work of contemporary historians such as Hartwell and Taylor.

If, as Jan Tinbergen states, it is really the differences in the earning power of trained and untrained workers that is the biggest reason for the income differentials in capitalist societies, then surely the supply of, and demand for, untrained workers must be the determining factor. The differences in income would be less marked if the economy were to change from labor-saving, capital-intensive techniques to labor-intensive ones.

That certainly isn't about to happen in the industrialized world. As a result of rapid technological change, automation, and the growing use of industrial robots, untrained workers in industrialized countries will soon be faced with a choice between becoming better-trained or accepting less demanding and correspondingly less-well-paid jobs. As this phenomenon has more to do with technological progress than with capitalism, it applies to countries with socialist governments as well.

Capitalism, working in tandem with democracy, tends to create a permeable society, since it breaks down the barriers of class and of political allegiance. One's origins still have some bearing on career, of course, but training opportunities and a determination to work are of far greater importance. Capitalism fares well in comparison with socialist systems, which insist on taking political and ideological criteria into account when hiring new people. This is hardly surprising, for capitalism constantly creates new places at the table where the growing cake of prosperity is being consumed, without driving from their workplaces those who have already succeeded. In almost all cases where growth is lacking, however, rigid boundaries rise up between levels of society; hierarchies ossify, and there is a complete lack of social mobility.

EQUALITY OF OPPORTUNITY, NOT EQUALITY OF OUTCOME

It seems to me that equality of opportunity is more important than the coveted goal of getting rid of differences. Those differences are inevitable, frankly, given varying abilities, motivation, and circumstances. No assumption is more dangerous than the one that assumes that everyone in the economic sector has received the same abilities. Equality of *opportunity*—both desirable for the system and acceptable to everyone—should not be confused with equality of *outcome*. In my opinion, the tendency to hammer down above-average people is a perversion of the notion of social justice.

No one would deny that the "destructive creativity" of the market causes hardship cases. The welcome act of freeing individuals from the vague duties of precapitalist society and integrating them into freely chosen contractual agreements was one of the very conditions that enabled the capitalist system to make a breakthrough. People who have trouble standing their ground in a competitive economy were pushed to the edge of society then, and they still are now, because familiar attachments (local or institutional) have grown weaker. Carrying such people along within a socially acceptable framework is an ethical duty with which I am in absolute agreement and which, moreover, reinforces the legitimacy of the system as a whole.

In a democracy, we all must constantly strive to accept every living arrangement that is made, including the economic ones. Despite their often grotesque inefficiency, those compulsory measures prescribed by government such as pension plans, health benefits, and so forth, do to a certain extent attenuate the swings of the pendulum, and prevent society's differences of income and lifestyle from becoming simply too great.

Owing to the free-market system's incomparable ability to produce wealth, we can afford to pay for the building of consensus. Then too, the "welfare net" serves to attenuate all moral criticisms of capitalism and to prevent the formation of an anticapitalist majority. "The market delivers rough justice. The welfare state takes the roughness out of justice," says George F. Will, meaning, like Friedrich A. von Hayek, that in the final analysis the concept of justice is irrelevant to the functioning of the market mechanism in the end. It is not irrelevant, however, to most citizens, who have a natural tendency to demand justice from schools, churches, the government, and employers.

In view of the current inflation of demands made on the market economy, it is probably a hopeless undertaking to try to define *justice*. The market economy has become a victim of its own success, and who would not be pleased by that? Quite apart from our proclivity for applying "pure" doctrine to the complex problems of everyday life, we all realize that things only very rarely are black or white. And after all, who would complain of the fact that the industrialized countries of the West have now given almost everyone the chance to overcome life-threatening, crisis situations?

Admittedly, the free-enterprise system sets limits on social benefits and on the introduction of constantly new mechanisms for the redistribution of wealth (which are being exceeded in some places already). "The danger of people being degraded to [the station of] obedient pets in the state's stable," which Wilhelm Röpke warns us so forcefully against, also carries with it the risk of constant government intervention in the relations between labor and management. Cementing in place unproductive and unprofitable structures is in the interest of no one in the long run, and social hardship can never be outrun when the liquidator is standing at the door. Without going so far as to accord to social consensus the status of a fourth production factor, I believe that widespread acceptance of our economic system by the public remains vital.

Today, it is harder for opponents of the free-enterprise system to criticize it for a lack of efficiency than it was a few years ago; its contribution to the free organization of cohabiting nations is hardly contested anymore. Current criticisms and doubts more often are aimed at the moral and ethical dimension of the market; along with egalitarian pipedreams, the market's supposed failure to spread altruism is brought into play so as to weaken the system's appeal.

The struggle to create a consensus continues, and citizens' uncertainty—exacerbated by the fact that even our most respected moral authorities frequently display an unnatural lack of understanding of the ethical dimension of a market economy—only seems to grow. Certainly, the fact that many social encyclicals put liberal capitalism and communism on the same footing, in order to condemn both, gives me cause for misgivings.

The market economy does have a social component, in the broadest sense of the term, for it enables people to satisfy their basic human needs much more efficiently than all other economic systems. And it does so within a framework of government that gives the individual the greatest amount of room for self-actualization and for taking responsibility for his or her own life. As I have also made clear, it certainly is desirable to pay particular attention to the weaker members of society because this will help to ensure widespread acceptance of the system.

A final word of warning: overemphasizing that social component that can only be achieved by redistribution and leveling of income will of necessity lead to state tutelage, more bureaucracy, and a loss of freedom, thereby producing mainly costs, not profits, and acting as a brake on the free-market system's dynamic development.

13

The Global Vision for the Next Millennium

$\mathcal{C}$ertain words capture our imagination when they come into fashion. I feel ill at ease even writing them down, however, for these buzzwords lead us away from that levelheadedness and concrete, pragmatic thinking that we must have if we are to judge wisely and do what is right.

Vision is one of those current buzzwords, and therefore it should be used with moderation at first. Yet if such a concept leads more people to look beyond the present, to have a comprehensive concern for the future rather than just an interest in quantitative forecasts, then it will have done its work well.

"He who lacks vision," it is said, "can neither fulfill great expectations nor turn big plans into reality." Vision, in other words, is an executive task. Its power can scarcely be gauged, for it arouses people's enthusiasm, unleashes their energy, and turns their dreams into tomorrow's realities.

Here at Nestlé, to a greater and greater extent, our employees are being involved in a far-reaching, continuous manner in all questions pertaining to their jobs and workplace. This comprehensive inclusion of our employees in our operations extends beyond the so-called quality circles that have come to us from Japan, thus avoiding their slightly fanatical and almost religious connotations.

NEW ECONOMIC AREAS AND GLOBALIZATION

Globalization is accompanied by another important challenge to top management, the accelerating pace of change. Therefore, when one is selecting new executives, the applicant's capacity to "manage change" must be taken ever more carefully into consideration.

New orders of magnitude are being created by the globalization of companies and the creation of new economic areas such as Europe,

139

United States/Canada and Mexico, the Pacific basin, North Africa. The pressure on single countries to adapt is growing, as they realize that isolationism and protectionism will lead to economic stagnation in the long run. The free-enterprise system and democracy on the Western model are constantly gaining ground and being reinforced even further by recent developments in communication techniques. This is apparent not the least in the evolution of Eastern Europe, but also, in the medium and long term, in the developing countries.

All of these tendencies are bringing in their wake more comprehensive and global business strategies. For a long while now, Nestlé has had a worldwide industrial presence in over 60 countries, as well as sales operations in almost every country in the world. Over the past few years, Nestlé has made a greater effort to fill in "white spots on the map," i.e., China, Egypt, Pakistan. Comprehensive globalization has now entered the final stage.

The emergence of larger domestic markets and the worldwide tendency toward liberalization and cooperation mean that Nestlé will have to reorganize its production facilities, not just in its domestic markets but, in the long run, abroad as well. Economies of scale and specialized factories are becoming more and more popular. This means that production sites and sales points are being situated farther and farther apart.

Things were different when European products were being exported to developing countries or, later, when production facilities were opened in those countries. That increased the value added to products manufactured there—a trend that is continuing. Now, however, something completely different is taking shape: a greater separation between production and sales points, owing to the globalization of markets and to liberalization, which allows production sites to be set up far from where the products are consumed. To a certain extent, this sets limits to previous efforts to decentralize.

Globalization of habits of consumption is reinforcing this tendency: rather than average global consumption, there are now single global segments such as Coca-Cola, jeans, McDonald's, small-count lines for candy, and Nescafé. At the same time, regional and national habits of consumption are not changing, particularly in the food branch. Therefore the proper balance must be found between such regional and global conditions. Decentralized operations and global connections, as well as coordination, will become increasingly important to business success in the future. Countries can be rather roughly classified as either *industrialized* or *developing,* and there is a tendency to apply a different business strategy to each of those groups of countries.

In industrialized countries the range of products is constantly being enlarged and renewed as far as quality, freshness, and convenience are concerned, for consumers are more demanding. This results in a correspondingly greater segmentation of product lines. It is important, therefore, to take advantage of the opportunities for new markets that social changes create vis-à-vis purchasing power or eating habits. Here the key terms are *single-person households, out-of-home meals,* different schedules for family members, and women working outside the home. It is also important to react to the specific demands that specialized, growing segments of the population (for instance, the elderly, or athletes) make for new products, which correspond to consumer demands for healthier food or more leisure time.

A dual strategy needs to be implemented in developing countries in the future. On the one hand, we must meet the increasing demand for classic Nestlé products from a growing population with more purchasing power; first by increasing imports, then by producing locally and regionally as well as by raising the added value of our products—as far as the climate permits. On the other hand, Nestlé must produce products that employ local raw materials and correspond to local eating habits, and sell them at affordable prices.

DEMOGRAPHIC SHIFTS

The social upheavals in Eastern Europe, Russia, and China also offer new possibilities for the food industry. Moreover, huge demographic shifts can be expected in the next 20 to 30 years. Today barely 15 percent of Nestlé's sales are generated by the countries that contain 80 percent of the world's population. The importance of the great size of the populations in India, Nigeria, and Brazil, for instance, will be felt more and more.

Research—not just applied research but also, and especially, basic research—will be of ever greater importance to ensure that Nestlé's different business strategies take on concrete form and are implemented. Perhaps such research will lead to the creation of completely new types of products, unimaginable today. Research is also an important way of combating environmental problems. Growing problems (for instance, in the area of packaging) are being met with progressive solutions, owing both to an exponential increase in environmental awareness and to technological advances.

As a result of increased purchasing power and a growing population, volume sales continue on unhindered. Over the past few years Nestlé's sales have grown at the rate of between 3.5 and 4.5 percent, and there is no reason why this internal growth should not continue.

Until the turn of the millennium and far beyond, the growth in the world's population, and its consequences, will play a crucial role in human nutrition. According to the most recent calculations, population growth does seem to be slowing down; yet even the most optimistic forecasts do not foresee the rate of growth being reduced to the replacement rate of pre-2015. In other words, by around the year 2100, the world's population should be between 8 and 12 billion.

Therefore, mankind must find new ways to feed people; one example is the growing trend toward the replacing of animal protein with vegetable protein. Completely new prospects are opening up—and hopes taking shape—owing to the broad research efforts in the field of genetic engineering. Progress in this field could well lead to a solution for the problem of feeding the world's population. It would be more important and have greater consequences than the "Green Revolution," which was an indisputable aid to countries such as India, Indonesia, and the Philippines. At present a mere 1 percent of all known plants are used as food, and 20 to 30 percent of all food harvested is destroyed by insects, rodents, or rots before it can be sold.

THE WORLD IN WHICH WE LIVE

Cynics correctly maintain that "predictions are always chancy, especially when they concern the future." Nonetheless, there can be no business strategy without forecasts. As long as it is roughly representative in its broad outlines, a soundly researched and prepared strategic concept can weather the unavoidable damage, delays, steps backward, and even the errors of its authors.

An important element of any strategy, of course, is the judging of business conditions in the area where you hope to do business, for a strategy is meant to be implemented. Without donning the prophet's mantle, one can discern a series of tendencies and developments, reasonably likely to become realities. For a while now we have been moving away from the bipolar constellation that has influenced politics since the end of World War II, toward a tripolar system. Ideological conflict is being replaced by competition on an economic level, the lines of force running through North America, Europe, and Japan and the Pacific basin.

The reason for these developments is the collapse of socialist ideologies. That epic event has had an effect not only on the situation in Eastern Europe and Asia but also has had an impact all over the world. For some years now the authority and legitimacy of socialist theory had become increasingly difficult to defend to the democracies of the free world. As an ideal for economic activity, that theory had outlived its usefulness long before. Imminent political, economic, and environmental collapse forced the leaders of the Soviet Union to stop the arms race, to begin cooperating with the West, and to concentrate on their own internal problems. Astonishingly, in only a few days, the worldwide empire of the Soviet Union fell like the proverbial house of cards.

We may assume that the superpowers will increasingly choose to work together. That will mean a world with less tension, fewer and/or shorter wars, and smaller sums set aside for armaments. This certainly does not mean that all dangers have disappeared: the Middle East powder keg could explode at any time. Other potentially explosive areas are Eastern Europe and the Balkans, the countries of the former Soviet Union, and the Indian subcontinent.

Other countries are still changing their power structures or political systems. Over the long term it will be impossible to stop these changes; thanks to modern means of communication, liberal democratic ideas have permeated everywhere. The catastrophic failure of socialistic tutelage for the economy and for society, coupled with the undeniable successes of the free-market countries over the same period, will everywhere increase the pressure to adapt, even in Africa and Latin America. Marxism has had its day as a serious philosophic, sociopolitical, and economic doctrine. What Abraham Lincoln said has proved to be true: "You can't fool all of the people all of the time." Perhaps the world's bitter experience with socialist ideologies will help mankind to be a bit more wisely skeptical when it is faced with the next charlatan.

One of the first reciprocal effects of these political changes has made itself felt in the economy, which now is starting from a new position. One of the vital aspects of this new position is the importance that has been accorded to liberalizing the economy over the past few years. Mistrust of the all-knowing (and all-powerful) state has led to government pulling out of more and more businesses, or at least to its not increasing the number of regulations affecting business (and sometimes even reducing them) and, in general, to greater confidence on the part of government in the self-regulating mechanisms of the market. As a result, structures are being more rapidly adapted; productivity is growing, and competitiveness is improving.

Some developing countries with too many incapable bureaucrats, whose slow decision making was often a great hindrance to businesspeople, have recognized the danger and are trying to make improvements. At the same time, not the least under the impact of discussions of the foreign-debt problem, people are once again realizing the advantages of foreign direct investment. In places that a few years ago presented obstacles of every sort for the entrepreneur to overcome, the more far-sighted countries now are engaging in actual advertising campaigns to convince the former "evil multinationals" of the advantages to doing business in their countries. This is true even of regimes that used to vaunt their extremely populist, not to say socialist, economic policies.

Closer regional cooperation in the economic sector is catching on. The European Community, NAFTA between the United States, Canada, and Mexico, the still cautious groupings of Southeast Asian countries and those in the Pacific basin around their leader Japan, efforts in North Africa as well as in Latin America between Brazil and Argentina—all these are signs that the advantages of coordinating economies over a wide area have been recognized. And there seems to be some indications that, in Eastern Europe as well, the dissolution of Comecon will bring on real regional cooperation. The pressure of existing expectations in the area of commercial policy for currency questions shows that the fact of economic complexity is increasingly being accepted and its advantages for all concerned being acknowledged.

Despite all of the inevitable delays, structural problems, and difficulties in adapting, it will grow harder and harder for politicians of every stripe to advocate protectionism, dreams of autarky, or completely autonomous decisions with regard to commercial policies or exchange rates. I do not believe there is a future for rules about "domestic content," "voluntary limitations on imports," absurd financial aid for exports at the expense of the taxpayer, or any other such gimmicks.

Furthermore, I am convinced that this process of regional cooperation will accelerate markedly, because its advantages are obvious, and that the pressure of growing competitiveness will be felt in this area too. What this will entail for each company in general is, first of all, stiffer competition, with foreseeable consequences for strategy, size, and organization. We managers will have to get used to competing everywhere against other businesspeople from all of the world's economic regions.

On the other hand, we businesspeople will be able, much more often than previously, to invest our funds wherever they have the best chance to be effective; to purchase, produce, and sell, to obtain funds and pay wages and taxes, in places where we feel the conditions are most favorable. Over the longer term, however, global competition will cause all of the artificially produced advantages of certain locations to disappear. What will remain are those advantages resulting from the availability of natural resources and—a central factor—from the human and professional qualifications of the work force. Here is a job for representatives of the trade unions that, it seems to me, is much more urgent and important than complaints about "social dumping."

In the few remaining years before the turn of the millennium, some firms in every branch will stand out by virtue of their credible claims to be really global. Such claims must be backed up by more than just a certain volume of sales. International management and marketing experience also are needed, as is a range of products adapted to the needs and purchasing power of customers, a larger investor base, company presence on many stock exchanges, and experience in R&D, marketing, and production in many different geographic areas. Where more than the rudiments exist, companies often seek safety in alliances. In certain branches and cases, alliances are indeed a sound, pragmatic solution. In any case, they often are much more than just the best way out of a predicament, or a sign of last-minute panic.

Yet for me at least, there is no doubt that many of the transactions now being praised will not live up to expectation. Every joint venture, alliance, or cooperation agreement always entails some loss of freedom with regard to decision and reaction time—and that's the sore point. In the future the business outlook, methods, and systems, as well as competitors and organizations, will change more quickly than they now do. Furthermore, these changes will be more radical and far-reaching than they are at present, and each firm will have to face decision making that will have a real effect on whether it continues to exist. Timing is extremely important in such cases, and therefore, I would argue for keeping as wide a scope of action as possible.

In the future, businesspeople will be confronted with people who, in many cases, surely will not react as people do today. The loss of traditional values over the course of the twentieth century, with its long period of peace and prosperity in the West, has led to behavior that I would characterize as follows, without pretending to evaluate it.

Citizens, coworkers, customers, and investors are increasingly freeing themselves from a whole series of sociopolitical and job-connected obligations. They are becoming more concerned with somewhat narcissistic self-actualization, which involves concentrating more on one's own ego. Optimizing your own existence, even at the cost of your family's or society's existence, is no longer seen as being morally reprehensible. It will become more and more difficult to convince such people to volunteer to work at jobs that affect the common good, much less to work in the government or in political parties or simply to go and vote. A sort of creeping fundamentalism, a moral rigorism, accompanies this trend and makes it more and more difficult to weigh pros and cons rationally in, for instance, the case of environmental protection. At the same time, in many areas people are falling back on smaller units that are easier to grasp and to influence, on regional expressions and points of view that both provide a strange counteraction to the trend toward globalization and also to a certain extent limit its impact.

It would be presumptuous of me to deny that such tendencies also exist among our employees. Presumably, they will cause them to bring better professional qualifications into the company and to demand that their jobs be personally satisfying and provide guaranteed status and security, even while expecting from their superiors understanding, flexibility, and advancement—often while not being blindly loyal themselves to the company and its corporate culture. Like it or not, paternalism has had its day; our employees are more independent in their opinions and more skeptical with regard to traditional attitudes. A long-term commitment, be it to family, career, or politics, or even in the area of consumer conduct, depends for them on how well it fulfills clear-cut expectations. If these are betrayed—or even if they are seen as less desirable, for values are changing more rapidly—people are more liable to change. On the other hand, reorganizing or relocating a company, or changing work methods, no longer provokes the traumatic reactions that often made adapting to new conditions so difficult for people and so costly.

Today, Nestlé's shareholders (most of them already international in origin) do not behave as the company's investors once did. Increasingly they are institutional investors, with all that entails with regard to short-term thinking, capital structure, formation of shareholders' rights, requests for information, scope of expectations, and lack of personal relationship to the company. Their economic importance will increase, as will their tendency to take more direct steps to influence the company, with a view to increasing "performance" or to selling off the stock quickly when an opportunity presents itself.

In the future, it will be even more difficult than at present to classify our customers according to criteria based on their incomes. Their behavior will be characterized by spontaneity, opportunist considerations, and delight in experimentation. At the same time their standards will be higher: companies will be required to meet sociopolitical criteria that go beyond the product itself. A firm's conduct with regard to environmental protection, for example, or the perception of its "social responsibility," will be judged and sanctioned by self-consecrated authorities outside the firm—or even by enemies of the company. The motivation and composition of such groups often change; what does not change is the firm's interest in preemptively working on these topics with consumers so as to avoid having to mount one salvage campaign after another.

The working day of our employees and customers, like their working time over a lifetime, will no longer correspond to the structures we know today. Some of the elements that will contribute to destructuring our traditional conception of time are the following:

- □ The longer and longer amounts of time people will devote to education and training, while probably giving up a fixed age for retirement. (Either in deference to the individual's free choice, or because industrialized countries will need to innovate when the unfavorable age structure of their populations becomes too burdensome.)
- □ The growing proportion of women at every level of the business hierarchy.
- □ The introduction of more flexible working weeks, based on the fact that, as the cost of investments constantly grows, the capacity of production facilities continually needs to be improved.
- □ Continuing growth in purchasing power, coupled with more leisure time and longer vacations, which must be better spread out over the year if the infrastructure is not to be overloaded.

The process of demographic change, which has modified our world more far-reachingly in the last two decades than in the previous three centuries, will continue. Although it is dangerous to try to extrapolate from existing trends, human reproductive behavior does seem to be extremely resistant to innovations based on medical technology alone.

Though it fails to factor in a whole series of possible technological and political leaps, this is a rough outline of the world to which we businesspeople will have to adjust and in which we shall have to attempt to be successful.

For many years now, Nestlé has been literally a global company. Its more than 400 factories in countries throughout the world, from Argentina to Zimbabwe, from the People's Republic of China to the United States of America, produce a wide range of provisions and fine foods that are sold almost everywhere in the world.

Recent events have made it possible for Nestlé to carry through its first projects in Eastern Europe, in countries that formerly had state monopolies, and to make numerous contacts. This is the beginning of the last phase in Nestlé's globalization, which began shortly after the company was founded. The traditionally broad international support for Nestlé's industrial and commercial activities has, over the past few years, found an equivalent among our shareholders. More than half of Nestlé's shares now belong to international investors. Employees from 52 countries work at Nestlé's headquarters, and half of this Swiss company's management are foreigners.

The new order of magnitude of regional domestic markets and economic areas compels people to adapt. Companies make use of takeovers, subsidiaries, and strategic alliances to do so. This often produces a fait accompli, independent of planned regulatory or legislative measures, which contributes to the process's dynamism. For Nestlé this means reorganizing its production structure, not just in Europe but also further abroad in the longer run. In order to make as much use of "economies of scale" as possible, Nestlé is ready to separate production and consumption sites, something that is completely feasible today, thanks to computer technology. This closer, continuous collaboration beyond frontiers implies a rethinking of Nestlé's previous decentralization and the making of more team decisions within a specific economic area.

This tendency is reinforced by the formation of global habits of consumption, which are limited to certain segments, however. At the same time, regional and national habits of consumption, and consumer taste preferences, are being retained. Nestlé's success will depend, not the least, on how well it can work out a balance between regional and global elements. This extends far beyond the narrow field of products and, in the end, touches on the question of corporate organization. It seems to me that it would be wrong to give up decentralization, and just as wrong not to realize that it is in the company's interest to place more emphasis on coordination and closer connections.

In the industrialized countries, Nestlé will continue with its policy of constantly expanding and renewing its range of products. Contrary to the former widespread pessimism with regard to the chances for growth in the food industry in the industrialized world, Nestlé has observed that consumers remain thoroughly receptive to advantages added to products in the areas of quality, freshness, and convenience. Today, consumers in general make higher and more diversified demands, which manufacturers try to meet by increasingly segmenting their range of products.

Social changes also provide new opportunities to gain market share in shopping and consumption: single-person households, out-of-home meals, differing timetables within the family, and women working outside the home. Finally, there are new products certain to satisfy the much greater consumer demand for products that are healthier and increase personal well-being. Food products that make use of the increasingly better-known interaction between food and health and that can help to prevent illness will appear on the market.

Most of the countries where Nestlé wishes to sell its products are not at all homogeneous, and all vary greatly in their cultural, political, and economic conditions. In general, Nestlé applies a dual strategy.

On the one hand, increased purchasing power and a growing population help the sales of our classic products. Historically, Nestlé met demand by importing; but even early in the twentieth century it started producing locally and regionally, when the supply of raw materials and the climate made that feasible. In the foreseeable future the relative proportion of imports from industrialized countries will tend to decrease, while the added value in industrialized countries will grow. On the other hand, in developing countries, Nestlé stresses production of products based on local raw materials. This makes them easier for the local people to afford and also meets specific local needs and corresponds to local eating habits.

TOMORROW'S MARKETS

The momentous shifts in demography also affect Nestlé's strategy. New concentrations of population will form in countries such as India, Nigeria, and Brazil. Within the foreseeable future we will need to find new solutions in order to provide enough food for a world inhabited by approximately 10 billion people. One means that I have already noted is to replace animal protein (meat, milk) more and more with vegetable protein (e.g., soybeans). Completely new prospects are unfolding, and hopes being awakened, thanks to broad research efforts in the field of genetic engineering.

This raises the question of the importance of research. Without its discoveries, the corresponding strategies could never be carried out. Nestlé probably is unique in the food industry in having an integrated R&D system, one that engages in both applied and basic research in the fields of human physiology, health, nutrition, and raw materials. Such a system is capable of creating types of products that we cannot even imagine today, especially in that gray area between preventive medicine and food products.

Moreover, research also plays a very important role in overcoming environmental problems. Awareness of the environment is growing exponentially. For Nestlé, this is particularly important in its bearing on the field of packaging. It is forcing us to look for new technological solutions and to consider their interaction with our biological product: food.

Employees in Nestlé's factories in the year 2000 will be faced with some completely new challenges. Nonetheless, we do not use the term "participatory management" in this context, since it is ideological and can be wrongly interpreted. What Nestlé prefers and practices is to include employees in a far-reaching and continuous manner in a discussion on all questions touching on their jobs and workplace.

Our junior executives are both open to contemporary trends and at the same time, because of stiffer global competition, under greater pressure within the firm. Therefore one of management's permanent jobs must be to constantly and intensively look after these people. The motivation of the lower levels of company staff is not the only thing that depends on this—it also affects how the ranks of future management will be peopled, for they are recruited from among those junior executives. This is reason enough not to let things on this level deteriorate into a state of inner abdication and resignation. The best way to prevent this is to carefully control the corporate climate, to use a direct, personal style of management, and above all, to manage the company credibly.

In view of the growing pressure of competition, companies that miss the boat with regard to major changes will be faced with the alternative of implementing innovations in a do-or-die manner, with all of the ensuing costs, or of accepting one competitive disadvantage after the other.

Faster, Thanks to Computers

The introduction of computer networks a few years ago has changed working methods and jobs. In the foreseeable future the changes will be even more sweeping and, above all, take place more rapidly. Our employees have to be prepared for this—a change in mentality cannot be carried out on command. In the end, companies will achieve results faster and better by proceeding cautiously and by respecting the individual's understandable fear of change, while not overloading his ability to adapt, than by engaging in big campaigns that employees' and junior executives' incomprehension doom to failure.

It is vital that employees be included in this process. It is the user, not the specialist, who has to make the decisions. And in view of the fact that this involves big investments to meet future requirements, it also seems to me necessary for top management to devote more attention to computers. For instance, Nestlé has installed them with top-level management and is working in all areas on two groups of projects, from planning production to telecommunications for the entire Nestlé Group.

The consequences and advantages of this approach are obvious, for a more efficient computer network makes it possible to check products and sales quickly. It provides the company with simultaneous access to data from markets, on trade, and from business partners, and thus enables it to react in time. More flexible and more rapid decision-making processes are a necessity, particularly given the much more rapid action in those markets that are competing globally. At the same time, a firm may be tempted to centralize company management and to limit the operational freedom of local managers.

This danger can be met by increased efforts at coordination and by including people with local responsibilities in the decision-making processes, as well as by personal contacts that awaken confidence. Technology must not become an end in itself, however. Merely playing technical games tends to obscure the qualitative dimension that can result from introducing and generalizing the use of computers.

Epilogue:
Looking at the
Big Picture

$\mathbf{M}$y thoughts on management have been laid out extensively in the preceding pages. They are all solid ideas, and they have worked well for me and for Nestlé. Yet, every leader, every CEO, every boss, from time to time needs to step back and look at "the Big Picture." This exercise gives the kind of strategic perspective that a multinational leader needs.

In Nestlé's case, the big picture is all about feeding the world and providing food and nutrition for an ever-growing population—today and tomorrow.

Concern about having enough to eat every day has played a decisive role in the history of mankind. Changes of sovereigns, migrations of nations, religious, social, cultural, technical, and demographic developments—more often than not, all were influenced by the dominating fear of hunger. The farther the evolution of mankind progressed, the better people were able to understand, influence, and, finally, control the relationship between weather and harvest, between storage, distribution, and consumption. Today, as far as we can predict, not even a greater change in climate than has ever previously occurred would bring on catastrophic famine.

The food industry had a very crucial role to play in these developments, for it prevented biological materials that could not be stored and preserved for long periods of time from rotting and enabled them to be processed into nonperishable, safe products. A purely mechanistic view of agricultural production is too shortsighted, and the complexity of the food branch, from farming to consumption, cannot be controlled by issuing ordinances—contrary to the hopes and wishes of many official dreamers. At the same time, however, people must realize that the often derided inability of the system to find a sensible middle course between overproduction and shortages only concerns relatively small quantities of food: 1.5 percent more milk produced by the EC results in spare powdered milk and "mountains" of butter; a 1.5 percent drop in the millet production at harvest time in an African country can mean a period of famine for certain groups of the population.

This unexpectedly complicated and extensive system—in the United States, for instance, the food sector has sales of $1 trillion, more than the automotive, petroleum, or computer industries—now already makes it possible for 5 billion people to be fed (many, admittedly, quite poorly). By the year 2100, the world's population probably will have doubled. Will it be possible to feed it? And if so, how?

Malnutrition and bad eating habits are still serious problems in wide circles of the population in developing countries. Even where enough agricultural goods are produced to satisfy the needs of the entire population, there is endemic malnutrition springing from poverty, lack of education, and rigid social structures. This primarily affects the more socially vulnerable groups, such as children and women. Experience has proved that keeping farmers in tutelage by paying overly low prices to producers or, worse, attempts to collectivize farmers, inevitably end in crises and starvation.

There is absolutely no reason to be panicked by the hysteria coming from certain circles about the supposedly deteriorating quality of modern products. Today, people in the industrialized world eat better, more safely, and have more variety than their ancestors did. The problem, if there really is one, is that we eat more, or even too much, and do ourselves no favor thereby.

It is true that it will not be possible to feed 10 billion people in the same way as people in the West eat today. Rather than continuing to rely on animal proteins and carbohydrates, we shall have to accustom ourselves to eating more vegetable-based foods, by reason of cost if nothing else. The technologies that will make this possible are already available in part, and others are being developed. These foods will be just as tasty and varied, and definitely healthier, than those we eat today.

In order to obtain reliable sources of nourishment (something mankind has been striving to do since prehistoric times), we will have to make use of all available technology and not let ourselves be confused by the pathological fear of progress evidenced by certain groups. For instance, there are very good reasons for utilizing irradiation techniques on certain products; genetic engineering can provide us with a crucial breakthrough when it comes to improving all kinds of raw materials. Should mankind give up these opportunities because they fail to conform to the ideals of some well-fed prophets of doom?

Thus, the future will be a time both of responsibility and of opportunity for the food industry—just as the present is. Year after year, Nestlé spends well over SFr. 600 million ($425 million) on R&D. Its expenditures in this area have increased sevenfold over the last eight years, and a third of that amount goes toward basic research. That shows as clearly as can be that Nestlé's policy is aimed at the long term. It also shows that the food industry needs to acquire more detailed knowledge of nutritional requirements and of the effect of nutrition on well-being, as well as a more complete knowledge of the raw materials it employs and of the possibilities for adapting and improving them.

There has been quite a bit of pessimism about the chances for growth in the food industry, but it has been proved to be groundless. New consumer demands constantly are creating new needs. In a few years' time there will undoubtedly be new products on the market that will help to prevent certain illnesses (osteoporosis, for example). And yes, people of all ages will continue to enjoy chocolate products, which always have had a universal appeal.

THE GLOBAL TREND

In the coming decades, the international food industry will be faced with a dual challenge:

1. A constantly growing population in the third world, and the concomitant problem of feeding the increasing number of people adequately and sensibly.

2. A stagnating or declining number of people in the industrialized world, coupled with specific nutritional requirements with regard to quality as well as corresponding physiological and nutritional effects such as overeating, diabetes, or food for the elderly.

In 1992, the global population reached 5.4 billion. By 2000, there will be about 6 billion of us. Within a relatively few years, 90 percent

of the world's population will be living in today's developing countries. Therefore the food industry must make a considerable effort to
expand its capacity to transform, store, and distribute processed food
in those regions. New discoveries in the fields of microbiology and
genetic engineering will stimulate advances in agricultural productivity. In addition, considerable progress already has been made in preserving, storing, and transporting agricultural goods. Furthermore,
big food companies like Nestlé constantly are marketing more and
more good-tasting plant-based products with high nutritional value;
these are less expensive and waste less energy to produce.

Therefore it is now possible for us to assume that high-quality biological foods will be easily available, and that they will cost less to
produce and to process. It is only in the exceptional cases that the
famine that today haunts wide regions of Asia and Africa is caused by
lack of useful agricultural land. Famine generally can be traced back
to the shortcomings of political and economic systems, to a lack of
capital and experts, to inadequate planning and fixing of priorities, to
an insufficient network of roads and distribution, to a lack of incentives for farmers to increase production, and to too little education.

In the industrialized countries, on the other hand, the next few
decades will see a qualitative rather than a quantitative increase in
the global demand for food. Here the food industry finds itself un-
dergoing a radical change from a production to a service industry. As
far as business activities are concerned, this means

- □ Strongly expanding meals outside the home;
- □ Encouraging the sale of "convenience" products;
- □ Changing the production of existing products so as to make
  them easier to use in kitchen appliances (the microwave oven,
  for instance);
- □ Selective choice of raw materials with carefully controlled
  "health" values;
- □ Producing food with specific dietetic characteristics for the elderly, or low-calorie products or foods enriched with vitamins,
  minerals, and proteins for people with special nutritional needs
  (already being sold to groups of consumers now as prophylactic
  health aids).

The food industry has more than just dietetic problems to solve in the industrialized countries. Fierce competition in every market is stimulating efforts to improve taste, quality, and convenience by making more and more use of modern technology.

The growing glut on the market, the marked price-consciousness of consumers when purchasing food, and the pressure from retailers—all these have led to very stiff competition in the industry. It becomes more and more difficult to raise prices because of rising costs. Symptomatic of this trend is the fact that the increase in production costs in the food industry over the past years has been consistently lower than the general cost of living. In a number of areas there is overcapacity, due both to planned expansion and to the replacement of older installations with more modern and efficient ones.

A gradual shifting of power to the food stores has occurred in the industry. The buyer now has more power. From the industry's viewpoint this development is economically advantageous at least at the start, since it leads to lower distribution costs, which in turn have a favorable influence on the development of prices. In the end the economy exists for consumers, and they profit from it as long as competition is not restricted by concentrations. More concentration in the retail trade, which results in fewer retail companies, does not restrict competition.

One need only look at what really happens to see how aggressively these competitors deal with each other, and what kind of pricing policies they practice. With regard to the food industry and its policies when supplying goods, the problem has more to do with the consequences of consumers' greater purchasing power (e.g., a wider range of discounts). Wholesalers and individual stores that do not belong to these big groups are subject to unjustified discrimination as a result of the range of discounts. It also becomes more difficult for new parties to enter the market.

Generally Nestlé has responded to this new situation by intensifying innovations and research, improving quality, and trying to enlarge its market share by marketing and advertising on the one hand and acquisitions on the other. Nestlé has tended to stress qualitative growth and a more cooperative—but not undignified—type of collaboration with retailers, greater support in publicity and marketing policies for differences in quality, while making use of streamlining and lower costs to attack those problems on the level both of marketing and of costs.

On the other hand, the food industry in general gradually will learn how to better differentiate between products, quality, service, and brands, while simultaneously taking more efficient measures to lower costs. The result will be that differences in prices that are acceptable to consumers will correspond more closely to the actual differences in costs between generic products, store brands, and national brands.

As a result of all of this, brand-name manufacturers—or at least that part of the industry that is efficient and has good positions on the market—once again will be able to maintain and expand their market share. For the others it will become increasingly difficult—but that is true, in general, for the entire economy. Things will become more balanced in the future, the conflicts between industry and the retail trade will die down to a certain extent, and once again people will start to pay more attention to marketing.

About the Author

German-born **Helmut Maucher** is Chairman and CEO
of Nestlé, the world's largest food company. He assumed
the top post at the Swiss company in 1981, and since
then has gained a reputation as a straight-talking
industrialist who takes undisguised pleasure in going
against the established wisdom. This has brought about a
certain degree of success: in 1993, Nestlé achieved sales
of $38 billion.